Finding
the Angel
Within

Finding the Angel Within

Spirituality, Body Image, and Self-Worth

Pamela H. Hansen

DESERET
BOOK

Salt Lake City, Utah

Library of Congress Cataloging-in-Publication Data

Hansen, Pamela H.
    Finding the angel within : spirituality, body image, and self-worth /
Pamela H. Hansen.
        p.   cm.
    ISBN-13: 978-1-59038-865-5 (pbk.)
    1. Spiritual life—Church of Jesus Christ of Latter-day Saints.
2. Body, human—Religious aspects—Church of Jesus Christ of Latter-day
Saints.   3. Self-esteem—Religious aspects—Church of Jesus Christ of
Latter-day Saints.   I. Title.
    BX8656.H365 2008
    248.8'6—dc22   2007051572

Printed in the United States of America
Worzalla Publishing Co., Stevens Point, WI

10   9   8   7   6   5   4   3   2   1

To Mark, my eternal sweetheart

Contents

Acknowledgments

I want to thank Jana Erickson at Deseret Book for the insight and encouragement she has provided for this book. I also appreciate Richard Peterson, whose edits have been especially helpful. I feel very fortunate to enjoy their friendship as well. Thanks also to Richard Erickson for his design talents and Tonya Facemyer for her typesetting skills, as well as to the rest of the Deseret Book and Time Out for Women team. Rosie Jackson and Rachel Higginson are great friends as well as colleagues, whose talents, ideas, and support have helped to inspire those with whom we work. I also wish to thank those who have read various parts of this manuscript. The feedback has been very useful and much appreciated.

Thanks also to my dear husband and children, who have been very patient during this whole process. They continue to be my inspiration. To my extended family, friends, and my sweet ward sisters who have encouraged me to keep writing, I offer my heartfelt thanks.

I am especially grateful to all who have shared their stories with me, which have brought tears of sadness as well as smiles of joy. Each of those I asked to share their personal accounts in this book gave me permission to do so. I understand how difficult it is to share tragedies as well as triumphs, but I also recognize the comfort it can bring to others.

Just one more thought: I don't know that I'll ever really look like the lady on the cover; but I can imagine how she feels. There is hope, joy, and peace in that feeling—that can come through the concepts I have hoped to convey in these pages.

CHAPTER ONE

Finding the Angel Within

While taking a walk one beautiful cool morning, I was thinking about the message I hoped to share through this book. I wanted to show just how important it is to listen to the whisperings of our Father in Heaven with regard to the divine beauty of the human body. Although that voice is clear, it's seldom loud, and if we don't listen carefully, many of us run the risk of missing the message and becoming confused. Perhaps this is because the worldly voices are shouting so much louder.

Based on correspondence I have received and discussions I have had with many women, it is clear that a lot of unhappiness results from agonizing over our physical appearance. But I have also learned that if we are able to hear the divinely inspired messages about our wonderful mortal bodies, we can find a serenity and peace that elude those who are caught up in the world's obsession with the so-called *ideal* body.

This obsession is evident in advertising. Popular magazines, television, the Internet, and billboards all celebrate the beauty of the human body; however, there is usually a "certain type of beauty" that is held up as an example. And the *ideal* body image portrayed is so attractive and enticing that we want to believe their message—that looking like those beautiful models is necessary for acceptance, success, and happiness. After all, given a choice, who wouldn't like to look like that?

I have also learned that if we are able to hear the divinely inspired messages about our wonderful mortal bodies, we can find a serenity and peace that elude those who are caught up in the world's obsession with the so-called ideal body.

One of the things that has occurred to me while thinking about this topic is that much of this advertising is basically dishonest. Do you suppose that when the manufacturer of a hair product or skin treatment (or more to the point, his advertising agent) wishes to portray the benefits of that product, he finds a girl or woman who has drab, dead-looking, colorless hair, or blotchy, rough skin, has her use the product until it works its magic, *then* photographs her? Or isn't it far more likely that they find a girl or woman (a model) who *already* has a beautiful thick head of hair or a peaches-and-cream complexion to use in their ad campaign? Then there is something called an airbrush that can be used to further enhance the image. Perhaps that's why it often says in small print: "results may vary."

The reality is that except for the relatively few women who look like that "naturally," the rest of us come up short to some degree. And without spending inordinate amounts of time and money to achieve such a body or without submitting to extensive cosmetic surgeries, we are never going to have what the world defines as an ideal body. Most of us would have to give up so much in other areas of our lives to achieve the ideal appearance that our lives would quite literally fall apart. That isn't to say we shouldn't spend time and effort to ensure a healthy lifestyle. There are aspects of our appearance that we can and should seek to change, and much of the information we receive from knowledgeable sources in the world can be helpful in this regard. But if we pay attention only to what the world says, not pausing to stop and listen to the still small whisperings of the Spirit or ignoring the revealed truth about our eternal selves, we can easily get distracted by an impractical and futile quest. Focusing on worldly achievements and acceptance has never been the way to true happiness, and an obsessive discontent with our physical appearance can lead to unhappiness if not despair.

> Most of us would have to give up so much in other areas of our lives to achieve the ideal appearance that our lives would quite literally fall apart.

Once, when I was expressing my frustration at having so many things to do, so many places to go, and so little time, I was thinking about the lessons I have learned during the past few years. One of the most important things I have learned is that I need to pause occasionally to rejuvenate—physically, spiritually, and emotionally, although not always necessarily in that order. I had to be honest with myself. I wasn't doing that like I knew I needed to do.

I thought I'd learned lot a on the subject of my physical body. I realize I've had quite a tender education over the years from a wise and loving Heavenly Father, but I discovered that I needed a little—okay, a lot—more practice. And what an education I continue to receive!

The past two decades of life have been a wonderful mix of joy and sorrow, trial and triumph, for me. It hasn't been until recently, when I have been able to step back and see the "big picture" of life that I have realized how precious the difficult times are because of all they teach us. Life can be pretty tough, downright brutal at times. It isn't easy for anyone. It wasn't meant to be. We all have trials. In hindsight it is easy to see how lovingly, individually tailored those trials are even though they can be so grinding at the time. For many, the first inclination may be to tell ourselves to "buck up and keep moving!" At the other extreme we may be tempted to stall and wallow in self-pity. However, I have come to realize that there is an important middle ground between simply bucking up and wallowing in hopelessness. I call this middle ground the season of "tender care"—a time when we are able to heal by taking a healthy dose of love and patience for ourselves.

> Focusing on worldly achievements and acceptance has never been the way to true happiness, and an obsessive discontent with our physical appearance can lead to unhappiness if not despair.

In *Running with Angels*, I wrote about the challenges our family has faced over the years, the way I responded to those challenges—for better or for worse—and how I've tried to move on in life. In response to that book, many wonderful people have generously shared tender, sometimes heartbreaking, stories of their losses, recoveries, and triumphs. This notion of tender care is a common thread running through most of these stories.

After going through one of life's significant trials, most

people seem to need time to deal with the initial shock. Many have described how they wandered for a time, struggling to simply "buck up," and sometimes falling into self-pity. Most eventually come to a realization that the best way to put the trial behind them is to allow themselves a measure of tender care. People tend to find a surprising inner strength to forge ahead when they learn to embrace a sense of love and patience for themselves.

I have come to realize that there is an important middle ground between simply bucking up and wallowing in hopelessness. I call this middle ground the season of "tender care"—a time when we are able to heal by taking a healthy dose of love and patience for ourselves.

The trials and challenges I wrote about in *Running with Angels* taught me some important lessons about the wonderful angels in my life and about myself. There have been other challenges since, and I suspect there will continue to be challenges if the lives of everyone I know are any indication. Looking back, I can honestly say that my life is much richer for having endured some significant troubles. I am now profoundly grateful for events and circumstances that I once viewed as horrible tragedies. I am grateful for the lessons these experiences taught me. Even more, I am grateful for the important bonds that have been strengthened in my life—bonds with Heavenly Father, the Savior, my husband, my children, my extended family, and my friends have all been enriched and strengthened in ways that would not have been possible in the absence of these difficult experiences.

I have asked others who have experienced life-altering

hardships if they would be willing to give up any of the challenges they have endured. They hold dear the lessons they have learned, having purchased them at so great a price. That is the way I feel about my experiences as well.

The first several years of my married life seemed to be stereotypically blissful. My husband and I were both students. We had good jobs. Three weeks before I graduated from college, we had a baby boy, Nicholas, who was the joy of our young, relatively carefree lives. About two years later we decided to expand our family, and we soon discovered that I was carrying twin girls. We were thrilled! Several weeks later we learned that one of the babies had a fatal heart defect. And thus began a series of challenges that would shape our lives in painful but wonderful ways. Emily and Amy were born on a cold February day. Emily lived for almost 24 hours. Amy was a source of joy and comfort during that very difficult period. I struggled with the process of mourning Emily's death, bonding with Amy, and mothering Nicholas. Fortunately, I had help from many wonderful earthly angels—my mother, my grandmother, my mother-in-law, sisters, sisters-in-law, and numerous loving and concerned neighbors and friends.

People tend to find a surprising inner strength to forge ahead when they learn to embrace a sense of love and patience for themselves.

Two years later, Sarah was born. She was a healthy, happy baby. However, at about 18 months of age, she began to limp and favor one foot. After more than a year spent visiting a wide variety of doctors, it was determined that Sarah had juvenile rheumatoid arthritis. Although she struggled with that disease throughout her childhood, she has been symptom free for almost four years now. She has come a long way, and we are overjoyed. We are certainly grateful to live in an age where there has been competent medical help. It hasn't been easy for her, but she is doing great!

Stephen was born three years later. He has enjoyed relatively better health. A few trips to the emergency room or doctor's office for a sports injury, while thrilling in the moment, pale in comparison.

Our next child, Hillary, was born a little over three years later. When she was about 18 months old we discovered a lump on one of her fingers, which turned out to be a bone tumor. She was diagnosed with Ollier's disease. She has

I am now pro-foundly grateful for events and circum-stances that I once viewed as horrible tragedies. I am grateful for the les-sons these experi-ences taught me.

several tumors growing inside her bones. When she was first diagnosed, we had no idea how mild or severe a case hers would be. But, as time has gone on, it has proven to be mild, and we are thrilled. There have been a few times over the years when we've been a little frightened by the disease. This past year she had to have some of the tumors removed. The tumors were sent to a lab to determine if they were malignant. The time spent waiting for those lab results seemed like an eternity! Fortunately, there were no cancer cells in the tumors, and I have been amazed at how her doctor used donor bone and marrow from her own hip to reconstruct her finger. Looking at her current X rays six months after the surgery, it was difficult to tell there was even a reconstruction done. Miracles are achieved every day at Primary Children's Medical Center!

About three and a half years after this daughter's birth,

Mark and I were on an evening walk. I asked him what he would think if I told him I was pregnant. He said he would think I was crazy because medical science said there was more than a 99% chance that I couldn't be pregnant. I told him we were that lucky one percent and that there must be a very good reason for this baby to come into the world. A few months later we made an appointment to visit with a genetic counselor and to have a detailed ultrasound exam to determine if the baby had any birth defects. We informed the genetic counselor ahead of time of the other health issues our children had experienced. When we met with him he told us that he had researched the several conditions in our family's history and that there was no genetic connection between the heart defect, juvenile rheumatoid arthritis, and Ollier's disease. He told us that, statistically, what we had experienced in one family shouldn't happen. We were apparently just very unlucky!

He told us that, statistically, what we had experienced in one family shouldn't happen. We were apparently just very unlucky!

Little did we know just *how* unlucky. We went directly from his office to the ultrasound exam room. There we learned that the baby had died. Several hours earlier I had felt the baby move. We couldn't believe it. We returned to our home and gathered the other kids and told them the news. We then went to the hospital where I was to give birth to a beautiful stillborn baby boy. The birth was a difficult one. We named the baby Eric.

Dealing with the deaths of our children as well as the medical conditions of our daughters had all taken a toll on my emotions and, as a result, my health. In my anxieties, I found eating to be a great comfort. It wasn't long before I weighed over 100 pounds more than when Mark and I were married. And after Eric's birth, I pretty much hit rock bottom emotionally.

The day we buried him next to his sister Emily was a chilly yet beautiful spring day. However, the sky didn't seem very blue. It was a dreary gray to me. As I described my feelings in *Running with Angels*: "Springtime was breathing new life into the cold, desolate ground, just as my world seemed to be crashing down once again. For days afterward, I felt physically and emotionally empty. I couldn't remember ever

> *In my anxieties, I found eating to be a great comfort. It wasn't long before I weighed over 100 pounds more than when Mark and I were married.*

feeling such an actual hollowness as I did then. The void seemed to permeate my soul. Although Eric had never taken a breath, I had felt life from him, and I still ached for this child" (p. 55).

Soon after burying little Eric, I was desperate to simply feel better. I wasn't hungry, and food didn't seem to be the answer. It seemed so inviting one morning to be outside, I decided to take a walk. It lasted only maybe five or ten minutes. I tried it again the next day. During those first few walks, I caught a small glimpse of feeling better, and that feeling of well-being grew as I made walking an essential part of my day. That precious exercise time, which I have since diligently tried to get six days a week, has resulted in another miracle in my life and that of my family. Many blessings have come from losing 100 pounds. So, too, has come the realization that the best way out, according to Robert Frost, "is always through."

When I was a teenager, I had a dream to run a marathon.

That dream was born the day I volunteered at the Salt Lake City *Deseret Morning News* Marathon with two of my friends. We stood at the finish line helping runners to the water and massage tables. It was seeing the triumph in the faces of the runners as they crossed the finish line that day that inspired me to make running a marathon my goal.

After more than a year of training, what a thrill it was to run that Salt Lake City *Deseret Morning News* Marathon in 2002! The next year I ran the St. George Marathon, which I did again in 2006. Each was terribly difficult but incredibly rewarding. I'd love to do another one!

And that's about where things stood when *Running with Angels* was published in 2005. I am thrilled to report that at this writing all our children are healthy and happy. We are deeply grateful for those blessings, but if I thought our family's health challenges were all in the past, I was mistaken. I hope you can bear with me for a few pages of update.

> *During those first few walks, I caught a small glimpse of feeling better, and that feeling of well-being grew as I made walking an essential part of my day.*

The next thing that came along was Mark's back problems. He had been living with the pain of three herniated disks for years, but one day a couple of years ago, the pain became severe. At about four o'clock the next morning, he rolled over in bed and felt something pop in his back. By the time the kids were up and getting ready for the day, I could see that Mark's pain was definitely getting worse. The practical side of me wondered if he could hang on just long enough for me to get the kids dressed and on their way to school. (I've felt somewhat guilty about that ever since.) He mumbled some sort of answer that I took to mean that he could wait.

After the kids were out the door, I quickly drove him to the emergency room, as by this time he had really convinced me that this pain was even worse than childbirth. It was terrifying to watch. We discovered later that fragments of two of the disks in his spine had broken off and had become lodged in the channel through which some of the nerves to the legs pass. He was in unbelievable pain. It took huge doses of painkiller to relieve his suffering even a little. Later in the day, after doing some tests, the doctor performed an operation, shaving off the bulging areas of two of the disks and removing the lodged fragments. Mark spent a few days in the hospital, but when he came home, although his back was relieved of the pain he had experienced, his left leg began to go numb, and he was also losing some mobility in that leg. We thought at first

This was my sweetheart, my buddy, the one who had always been there when I experienced such agony in the birth and loss of our children. He, who had always been the strong one, was now the one who was helpless.

that it was simply a natural result of the surgery and that it would gradually get better. Come to find out, the two disks had completely collapsed. Thus, five days after the original surgery, he was back in the hospital to have three vertebrae fused together. The second surgery was much more complicated and invasive than the first, and I was amazed at the medical technology of today, including the hardware installed in his back. But I was most impressed with the miraculous healing power of the human body as he began to get well.

For many years Mark and I had faced medical issues of our children. But we faced them together. Now I watched as he endured the pain, the uncertainty, the invasive repair of his back, the immense throbbing he felt, and although there were many loved ones around, I felt more alone. It was quite a strange feeling. I didn't think Mark was having much fun, either. This was my sweetheart, my buddy, the one who had always been there when I experienced such agony in the birth and loss of our children. He, who had always been the strong one, was now the one who was helpless. He was the one who had been there to put his arm around me and offer comfort. Now he looked up at me through eyes of pain and yearning for relief. Witnessing what he was going through, I often marveled at those who face heartache and challenge alone, without a companion. My heart ached for them, as I could feel just a little of their pain.

Mark's surgery, though not necessarily life threatening, was very intricate, and his recovery would take some time. In fact, when he came out of the hospital, he needed a lot of care for several weeks. It was a harrowing time for him, and he had been my main focus of concern for those weeks.

During that time, I hadn't paid much attention to a pain in my shoulder, which over several months had steadily become more severe. By the time Mark had been home from the hospital a few days, I realized just how much it was hurting. I could barely move my arm.

It was my turn to see the doctor, and he diagnosed a rotator cuff injury. I had let it go so long that it was beyond the point where a cortisone injection and physical therapy would do any good. And it was simply too painful to do much of anything. The doctor scheduled surgery a few days later for a rather routine scope of my shoulder. Mark and I were quite a pair, recovering together.

My recuperation time was a matter of weeks, and within just a few months I felt like a new woman. Mark, on the other hand, remained fragile for quite a while. We found there is no place for impatience in mending from major back surgery! It has been a long haul for him as he continues to heal. Although he is improving, we know some things will never be the same for him.

Although there may be intervals in the flow of the challenges of life, we are probably always going to have obstacles in our path.

I offer this update only to illustrate that although there may be intervals in the flow of the challenges of life, we are probably always going to have obstacles in our path. I base this conclusion not only on my own experience but also on the many stories I have heard from so many others. Their struggles have brought tears to my eyes. People have shared heartrending stories of the death of a baby or a close loved one, of a never-ending battle with weight, of a difficult surgery here, an inability to work there, an unfulfilled dream, and the list goes on; it is, I've concluded, all part of our marathon journey through mortality.

One of the things I have noticed in my own life and discovered in the stories people have sent me is that often it is our self-image that seems to suffer when we find ourselves swamped by the inconveniences and the disasters that life throws at us.

It is easy to listen to the messages of the world when we feel beaten down by life's challenges. Some of those remedies may sound inviting. Ironically, it is during those times that we most need to be listening to our Father in Heaven's messages about these wonderful human bodies we have.

As you might suspect, the running of a marathon has become a powerful metaphor for me. Though I have enjoyed running marathons, I realize that it's not everyone's dream. And that's fine (although they really can be incredible experiences!). I do believe, however, that metaphorically we are all running some kind of marathon in our lives. Perhaps it's one we actually want to run. Maybe it's one we don't want to run at all; but we find ourselves running anyway. Maybe we are resting, between marathons. Somewhere, someone is beginning a grueling run. And somewhere else, someone is completing theirs and realizing what a learning, motivating experience it is. Lessons learned in each marathon can help us in the marathons that will surely follow.

Providing tender care for ourselves requires two things: first, finding what individually works for us and, second, making the time to do it.

One of life's marathons that is difficult for many people, especially women—young and not so young—is that of forming a healthy body image spiritually and intellectually and then physically achieving a body to match. As with actual marathons, this marathon can be demoralizing at times and exhilarating at others. For many of us, this marathon is all about making changes—changes in outlook, attitude, and behavior. One thing is certain: In order to effectively seek and make changes, we need to allow ourselves a good bit of tender care.

Providing tender care for ourselves is a simple concept that can be very difficult to do, and yet is so necessary. It requires two things: first, finding what individually works for us and, second, making the time to do it. Often, as I have also experienced, many simply get so caught up in caring for others that they don't set aside the needed time to adequately care for themselves—physically, emotionally, and spiritually. Physically, taking a walk or getting some other kind of exercise can make us feel especially rejuvenated. So can relaxing by stopping in the middle of the day to put our feet up for ten minutes. Pausing to plan and shop for a healthy menu may seem difficult at first to do; yet it is greatly beneficial. Doing what we can to get plenty of rest can also make a huge difference in our lives. A bubble bath can make us feel a lot better, too. Turning off the radio in the car is a way we can tune out at least some of the noise. Of course if there is a van full of children along, nice soothing music may have a calming effect! Reading a good book is uplifting. So is quilting or painting or playing a musical instrument. Certainly immersing ourselves in the scriptures, personal prayer, and meditation can help us to spiritually care for ourselves. Finding what works for *us individually* is one of the keys to providing tender self-care.

Certainly if President Hinckley makes time for scripture reading as well as exercise, we ought to as well!

The second thing is to make time to do it. I was so impressed to hear during the time when President Gordon B. Hinckley was encouraging all of us to read the Book of Mormon by the end of the year, that two of the things at the top of his To-Do List each day were to read in the Book of Mormon and to exercise. He felt the responsibility to care for himself so that he could care for members of the Church. And he made time to do it. Certainly if President Hinckley makes time for scripture reading as well as exercise, we ought to as well!

It takes effort and courage to set that time aside. We may feel as though we are being selfish. But wouldn't we encourage others to efficiently care for themselves? Why should we show love and tender care for others and yet not for ourselves? It makes so much sense to do so.

And how do we know when it's working? I've found that as it gets easier to make time to exercise, the more desirable it becomes to eat healthy and spend time reading the scriptures. The resulting peace is sweet to experience, and that reinforces our determination to continue to take care of ourselves. When I quit making excuses and actually look forward to how I'll feel after a workout or a healthy meal, I not only feel better physically and emotionally, but I know that I am taking good care of this wonderful gift God has given me. *I can testify to that.* I have felt it so strongly in my own life that I want to share that concept with others. Oooh, I'd love to say I'm perfect in this area. If it weren't for all those bumps and potholes in the road! But after all, they keep me on my toes.

> *As we progress toward achieving this way of seeing ourselves, our hearts will be at greater peace and our knowledge will be enhanced by the companionship of the Holy Ghost. We will come to know for ourselves, and in turn, encourage others to find and cherish the angel within.*

Taking tender care of self is a way of finding the angel within. It will cause us to enjoy more happiness, greater success in our endeavors, and particularly, a sense of peace that can fill our lives.

This marathon task of forming and achieving a body image that is both spiritually sound and physically healthy may take a lifetime. But the pursuit of it has been so satisfying to me that I'm certain it is something I'll never abandon. I refuse to give up. I have found, and I know others who have also come to dis-cover, that converting an attitude from one of indifference and hopelessness to honesty and anticipation will bring about a mighty change that has at its core a greater understanding of who we are, whose we are, and what our mission is here on the earth. As we progress toward achieving this way of seeing our-selves, our hearts will be at greater peace and our knowledge will be enhanced by the companionship of the Holy Ghost. We will come to know for ourselves, and in turn, encourage others to find and cherish the angel within.

In thinking about how we can find that angel, I thought of my friends who serve on the Utah County Search and Rescue team. They have been out many times to help find someone who is lost; often in the mountains above Provo. And they have learned through experience that they are more likely to succeed if they follow a certain protocol. Here are some of their search and rescue guidelines:

- First, be prepared. Take necessary supplies, such as radio con-tact, a GPS device, beacons, and know night signs.
- Watch out for your own well-being. Then, watch out for and always stay with your team members.
- And, finally, do all you can to find and help the victim—the object of the mission.

This order of priorities is often difficult for the family of the victim to understand; but, as it was explained to me, the team takes great care to assure there will not be more victims as a result of the search.

Follow this basic strategy on most calls: Determine the nature of the problem by gathering available information then decide on plan of action and possible alternative. Carry out the plan. Continue to reevaluate.

These rescue guidelines were prepared for a physical search and rescue, but I see many parallels in our search for our divine body image. For instance, it is not often that we have only ourselves to look after. We're usually on a "team." Many of the guidelines listed above will apply as we search for and rescue our real selves. The one real difference in our search is that we are often both the victim and the rescuer. There are therefore two roles for us to play, and the process can get a little confusing. However, the more effective we are at rescuing, the less of a need we will have to be rescued. May you be blessed in your search as you look for the angel within!

CHAPTER TWO

Finding You're Not Alone

I discovered two interesting phenomenon in writing *Running with Angels*. First, while sharing some painfully personal stories in that book about my weight and the loss of our children, I wondered if there was really anyone else who felt the same way I had. I often questioned why I was choosing to share something so intimate in an open book. Aside from feeling a little push—no, a *big* push—to share this part of my life, I knew that this was the sort of story I would have liked to read during years of struggle. That's why I ultimately wrote it and received the wonderful help to get it published.

Second, after the release of the book, I was surprised to receive message after message expressing gratitude for sharing my story. A lot of those who phoned or wrote or e-mailed me said they felt as if they were reading many of their own words. I was, at first, flabbergasted. Really. I never expected to hear from so many who felt the same way I did. I was touched by one woman who wrote, "My husband and I found out recently that we will lose our baby girl at birth, due to a fatal condition. It is nice to know that there really is someone out there who knows how I feel. We feel strength and courage in this trial we are facing."

After the release of the book, I was surprised to receive message after message expressing gratitude for sharing my story. A lot of those who phoned or wrote or e-mailed me said they felt as if they were reading many of their own words.

Those who took the time to communicate all reiterated the same message—that they no longer felt alone. They felt supported. They felt as if someone else understood their feelings of turmoil. There was relief in their words. Even women experiencing trials other than losing a loved one or struggling through obesity were grateful to know there were others out there who shared similar challenges, and they felt comforted in that fact.

There is, I've learned, comfort to be found in sharing life's experiences. Perhaps it is because we feel less alone. Or perhaps there is something therapeutic in finding a sympathetic ear, someone who can listen, having been there and done that.

My friend Jana related a painful yet somewhat humorous story:

During a recent trip to Hawaii, my husband and I took a kayak trip that involved paddling several miles up a river and then hiking along a thick, forested trail that led to a waterfall. The pool of crystal blue water below the falls looked cool and inviting after the long hike. Being vain (and also not wanting to subject the other hikers to the sight of my mammoth thighs), I decided to swim wearing the board shorts I had put on that morning over my swimsuit. The only problem was that I had failed to consider what would happen when I then had to hike about two miles back to our kayak in wet board shorts.

By the time we got back to our kayak, a large, painful rash had developed on my inner thighs. Sitting didn't seem to be a problem, so we continued to kayak for another hour or two before we returned to the dock. By that point, my skin was so raw that trickles of blood ran down my thighs. I was humiliated. How could someone with thighs as gigantic as mine even consider doing what I had done? I told my husband that I would have to have liposuction before I could do anything more active than lay by the pool, but the next day he suggested that we go snorkeling since that didn't involve walking. The rash on my legs was still bright red, but I thought a day at the beach sounded fun, and I didn't want my husband's vacation to be ruined by a wife with enormous thighs. It wasn't until after I had run headlong into the ocean surf that I considered the effect of salty seawater on my raw skin. I screamed in pain as a wave tossed me back onto the rocky shoreline. I was embarrassed and disgusted with myself. My plan was to go home, go on a strict diet and exercise regimen, and never mention the incident to anyone.

When we returned home, our grown children came to visit and asked about the trip. I gushed about how beautiful Hawaii is and how much fun we had. My husband added, "Well, it was fun except for the board short rash." Immediately recognizing the problem, my oldest daughter said, "Did you hike in wet board shorts? That happened to me when I was in Hawaii." My youngest (size two) daughter added in surprise, "The same thing happened to me when I was in Africa. I had to walk with my legs not touching for a week."

As I have come to find out, many of my female friends and family have experienced something similar, but they were all too embarrassed to talk about it. Each of us had jumped to the conclusion that the problem was the size of our thighs—not the effect of stiff, wet shorts rubbing against tender skin in a humid climate.

> *Maybe our pain is the consequence of a choice we have made. Or perhaps our suffering is simply the result of being human and going through the difficulties that are a natural part of mortality. Whatever the challenge, there are many of us who feel alone in our pain.*

Walking in wet shorts can be painful, embarrassing, and have long lasting effects. But how often do we limp along in pain, embarrassed and assuming we are the only ones who have ever suffered from other kinds of soreness? Maybe our pain is the consequence of a choice we have made. Or perhaps our suffering is simply the result of being human and going through the difficulties that are a natural part of mortality. Whatever the challenge, there are many of us who feel alone in our pain. One sweet woman poured out her heart to me, telling me much of what she had endured and said that for a long time she had thought no one else could understand how she felt. She wrote, "We often feel that we are the only person in the world to have such experiences, pain, thoughts, fears, and challenges."

One of the big problems about making assumptions about ourselves and others is that it can lead to feelings of isolation. And feelings of isolation can lead to negative feelings toward ourselves.

As we make these assumptions, we often wonder "Why?" I have asked myself this question, and I know countless others have as well. "Why do I have to go through such challenges? Why doesn't anyone else have to go through this, too? There are even feelings of "Why do I have to have size 10 feet?" "Why can't I go to Hawaii?" " Why does she get to have natural blonde hair, and not me?" "She eats twice as much as I do—and she never gains an ounce!" "Why are their kids turning out that way?" "Why aren't mine?" "Why is Heavenly Father 'making' me experience these painful times?"

It gets worse when we assume we are somehow being punished. Maybe we're certain that we don't deserve better. We question our abilities. It can add up to seriously questioning our value.

It's also easy to make assumptions about others, and usually we don't have all the information. Take an experience I recently had at the grocery store. I saw a sweet young woman with her mother. I know them quite well, and they were standing halfway down one of the aisles with their backs to me. I noticed that this young woman was wearing a shirt with spaghetti straps—something I hadn't seen her wear before. I wondered if I should go up and say hello or just pretend I didn't see them with her dressed that way. Now as I write it, it all seems a little silly. But it felt a bit awkward at the time. I decided to go ahead and say hi. The minute she turned around I could see why she was wearing the shirt. She'd had an allergic reaction, and she had a horrible rash all over. I could tell she felt miserable. The least little bit of clothing irritated her skin. She and her mother were on their way home from the doctor's office, and they were picking up a few needed items.

What if I had continued to assume this young woman had just decided to start dressing that way? That thought might have included, "Oh, wow—she's starting to go over the edge. I'm not even going to talk to them." And the one I've heard so many times, even from my own lips, I'm afraid, "I would *never* let my daughter dress like that!" I am glad I have grown up enough to realize that even if she had chosen to dress that way that day, it wasn't going to stop me from being friendly.

It reminds me of the time we were on our way to church, and I turned to one of my teenage daughters and noticed how short her dress was. I was horrified. I had always taught my girls to dress modestly, and this dress was definitely too short. And I was the one who had bought it for her! After thinking "How is this going to make *me* look," I tried to brush it aside. But I was all ready to give her "the talk" again. While on our way to church, where we learn about living happily as eternal families, I was ready to jump all over her with my modesty speech. Then my daughter said, "Mom, all my dresses are starting to fit this way!" She had been in a growth spurt, and it was past time to think about getting her some better fitting clothing. My first reaction was one that, had I expounded on it any more, could have caused feelings of isolation in both of us. I had jumped to a hasty conclusion.

It is easy to make snap judgments about the actions of others and jump to wrong conclusions. I remember times at the grocery store when I was so conscious about what others saw me putting into my grocery cart. I assumed they were having negative thoughts as I'd put something other than fruit, vegetables, or whole grains into the cart. Thinking back on it, I wasn't necessarily judging them by their own grocery buying habits, I was misjudging many of them by assuming they were judging me.

How much energy do we waste, assuming others are thinking ill of us? And how much better off could we be if we channeled that energy into something positive!

How much energy do we waste, assuming others are thinking ill of us? And how much better off could we be if we channeled that energy into something positive! Since that period of much emotional growth in my life, I have, on a few occasions, made a conscious effort to take note of my thoughts as I watch others at the grocery store. Wow. That sounds like I don't have near enough other things to think about. But I wanted to experiment to see if I had progressed since my earlier shopping days.

What I experienced most was positive. As I watched others and took note of their groceries, I realized a time or two that there was an item I had forgotten to get. I also recognized, with great relief, that it no longer mattered what others thought about the food in my cart. Granted, there are now more healthy items, but the weight of being overly concerned about what others think has been greatly lifted.

The example may be a simple one. But it illustrates how we assume various thoughts of others and jump to conclusions based on those assumptions, though they simply may not be true. I smile as I think back to Jana in her wet board shorts. She mentioned there were other hikers who may have seen her walking back to the kayak. While she was concerned about how she appeared to them, I wonder how many of them might have been thinking, "Ouch! I've hiked in wet board shorts before. I know just how that feels." Or perhaps they were even thinking, "Wow. Even a lady with cute little thighs can get the dreaded board shorts chafing!"

It felt good to read her words: "I am happy for you because now you can love yourself as much as we have always loved you!"

I received a sweet note from one of my best friends after she had read about my struggles in *Running with Angels*. She wrote how she had never looked at me the way I had often seen myself for many years. And it felt good to read her words: "I am happy for you because now you can love yourself as much as we have always loved you!"

Susan's story illustrates how we can often misjudge others and the pain we inflict by doing so:

My struggle has been with infertility. For many years my husband and I endured invasive and very expensive medical treatments and surgeries. I had two extremely severe conditions that made it unlikely we would ever have children. Month after month my heart would break as the treatments continued and the tests were always negative. This is a tender trial and easy to misjudge or not comprehend (as any trial is unless you experience it).

While I was going through this, all I wanted to be was a mother. I made a decision, however, to use my time wisely and pursue a graduate degree. I became a business woman and represented a large organization. However, I felt as though my career and degree meant nothing to others as they discovered I had been married for several years with no children, just other accomplishments. Some poor souls tried to convince me that I was on the wrong path and that I shouldn't put other desires in front of a family. Their reprimand of me was met with tears and an explanation that we had been trying for years. I know they felt badly for having been critical.

Although I loved my career, I yearned for little ones, and at times I would cry at night, wondering why my greatest desire had to be my greatest trial.

I was approaching 30, and I knew my biological clock was ticking. Some doctors were beginning to say that we would never have children. I finally, however, found one that was full of hope. After working with him for some time, he suggested a very expensive procedure, which we tried. The morning that I went to find out if it had worked I knelt down to pray and a voice spoke to my heart that said, "It will work this time, but you can't forget what you have learned by this trial." I was amazed to receive such a distinct answer, and I was tempted not to believe, since my heart had been too hopeful too many times. It did work and I had my twins a few months later.

I can recall times when my heart absolutely ached as I would hear other women talk about raising twins, while I was denied that particular opportunity in this life. I know some of the pain, disappointment, and the discouragement that is involved when you yearn for a child and such an earthly prospect looks dim or is denied you.

Susan's story has a happy ending. Just as happy, I think, is the fact that she has not forgotten what she has learned through her trial. I met Susan, along with her husband and their two darling boys, on the day of one of the Running with Angels 5K races. She said of her experience that day. "I ran with my angels, who, at one time, I thought I would never have."

> It can be downright scary to share of ourselves, and we often feel vulnerable to the judgments of others. But there is real power in sharing and in feeling the support of other people.

Two important lessons can be learned from Susan's account. One is the pain that is caused by jumping to conclusions and making faulty assumptions. The other lesson is how helpful and comforting it can be to others when we share a story of hardship. That's why I am so grateful to those who have given me permission to report their experiences in this book. When we open up a little about our own struggles, we not only feel less alone, but it encourages others to open up about their own trials.

I guess I have always known, in a superficial way, about the challenges life brings to others. But in the letters I have received, I have discovered how widespread human suffering is. Equally amazing is the discovery that when we are willing to open up our hearts and share our feelings, it is a helpful, sometimes life-changing thing to others. Moreover, there are many wonderful people who are ready to lend a listening ear, open a compassionate heart, and extend supportive, caring arms. It can be downright scary to share of ourselves, and we often feel vulnerable to the judgments of others. But there is real power in sharing and in feeling the support of other people.

Through their listening ears and understanding hearts, sympathetic souls are willing to put their arms around us and give us encouragement. Such comfort can also be a tremendous boost in the way we think about ourselves.

I'm not trying to promote gossip over the back fence or encourage discussion of all your troubles with the rest of the world. But I have found that in opening up to a trusted family member or friend, we can receive strength. How comforting it is to be able to have someone else help lift our burdens! Just to know there are those who will not judge or criticize but who will stop along the way with us and carry some of the load can be a tremendous relief.

Referring to the Holy Ghost, Jesus promised us that He will not leave us comfortless (see John 14:16–18). In addition to that divine support, comfort often comes through others. I like to call them "earthly angels." President Spencer W. Kimball perhaps had this in mind when he said, "God does notice us, and he watches over us. But it is usually through another mortal that he meets our needs. . . . So often, our acts of service consist of simple encouragement" (*The Teachings of Spencer W. Kimball*, ed. Edward L. Kimball [Salt Lake City: Bookcraft, 1982], 252). Through their listening ears and understanding hearts, sympathetic souls are willing to put their arms around us and give us encouragement. Such comfort can also be a tremendous boost in the way we think about ourselves.

It also helps when someone else experiences similar challenges and actually makes it through, enabling us to hope that we too can survive. We may be on the uphill side of our mountains, but when we see other "hikers" who have been to the top and are making their way back down, we are encouraged. The pain, however intense it may be, *will* pass.

I can find power and strength in sharing my feelings with others. I can also offer strength to others when I open my heart to their trials and really listen to them. Based on Jana's experience, if I get an opportunity to go to Hawaii, I will leave the board shorts home. And I'm reassured that in experiencing these earthly emotions and experiences, I do not walk alone!

Search and Rescue Tips

- Repeat these words as often as necessary: "I'm not the only one who has walked in wet shorts!"
- Ask: "Am I jumping to conclusions about or misjudging someone or a situation?"
- Try offering a smile and a simple "hi" to someone. That simple act can help someone feel as if they're not alone.
- Try opening up to a trusted family member or friend.
- Be a trustworthy and caring listener.

CHAPTER THREE

Finding Relief from Entrapment

As my son Stephen and I read together *Where the Red Fern Grows*, we learned about trapping a raccoon. In the book, soon after Billy bought his beloved hunting dogs, his grandpa taught him how to catch a "coon."

"You see," Grandpa explained, "a coon is a curious little animal. Anything that is bright and shiny attracts him. He will reach in and pick it up. When his paw closes on the bright object it balls up, and when he starts to pull it from the hole, the sharp ends of the nails will gouge into his paw and he's caught."

Billy was sure his grandpa was playing a joke on him, and he responded, "Why all he'd have to do is open his paw, drop the piece of tin, and he could pull it from the hole." But Grandpa went on to explain. "Once he reaches in and gets hold of that tin, he's caught, because he will never open his paw" (Wilson

Rawls [Garden City, New York: Doubleday & Company, Inc., 1961], 56–57).

Thinking about cute little raccoon paws caught in a crude trap isn't very pleasant, unless, of course, you're a boy in the Ozarks trying to teach your dogs how to hunt. The trap works because of the unwillingness on the part of the raccoon to let go of the shiny, attractive object that he wants so badly, not realizing that he could be free from the trap if he would only release his grip.

One of Satan's most effective strategies is to convince us that we need to look a certain way, be a certain size, and act in a certain manner.

How often do we find ourselves ensnared in raccoon-type traps set by Satan? He is vigorously using his most effective arsenal in devising methods to more effectively wear us down, tear us down, and pull us into his realm, and his hunting grounds are full of glitzy sparkle. We can better resist Satan's persistent ploys if we understand his motive for waging this war against us, "for he seeketh that all men might be miserable like unto himself" (2 Nephi 2:27). One of Satan's most effective strategies is to convince us that we need to look a certain way, be a certain size, and act in a certain manner.

One such subtle trap may be seen in elements of the fashion industry. Have you ever heard of "vanity sizing"? It is a term that is becoming more common these days. According to a study done on how women's clothing sizes have changed over the past sixty years, "vanity sizing," as it is called, is "a trend in which clothes are cut larger but labeled with smaller size numbers." April Ainsworth, owner of an on-line vintage clothing store, reported that people are not getting smaller, but manufacturers are lowering the numbers on sizes. "That's why a garment labeled size 12 in the 1950s might fit a woman who wears a size 2 or 4 today. . . . Shrinking sizes lead many women to falsely believe they may have dropped a size or two by their own merits, while in many cases that is simply not true." ("Clothing Sizes 'Shrink' to Boost Customers' Self-Esteem," by Lauren Waddell, *BYU Daily Universe*, 29 Nov. 2006).

It does not help that vanity abounds in our culture. A recent article in the *Chicago Tribune* reported, "Though the dress size of the average American woman is 14, the average fashion model is—you guessed it—a size 0 . . . Between the size 14 real and size 0 'ideal' exists a world of women and girls, many of them pursuing an elusive body type through means that can be psychologically and physically devastating.

Between the size 14 real and size 0 'ideal' exists a world of women and girls, many of them pursuing an elusive body type through means that can be psychologically and physically devastating.

"We feed the billion-dollar diet industry while denying our own bodies. We accept the premise that being thin will change our lives while failing to see that the pursuit of smallness, sometimes manifested in anorexia or bulimia, can actually shorten our life span . . .

"The truth is that loving oneself—and one's body—is a discipline all its own. It means challenging the images that the fashion industry has foisted on us. It means ignoring the voices that tell us that being healthy is a distant second to being thin" (Anne Ream, *Chicago Tribune*, 2007. www.chicagotribune.com/news/opinion/chi-zero_thinkju129,0,3904830.story).

Another trap Satan employs is to distort our perception of

the physical body by sending confusing messages, including calling good evil, and evil good. Like most of Satan's lies, what he promotes has a degree of truth, but if we accept these subtle falsehoods we can lose our way.

Another thing that tends to make us lose our way while trying to maintain a healthy perception about our bodies is fatigue. We are simply worn down in the struggle to resist all the false notions that are thrown at us.

This concept hit home to me one day as I was attending a conference with a friend. We were walking through the streets of an unfamiliar city, neither of us paying very close attention to the landmarks that would lead us back to our hotel. By the time we found the right street, we were quite thirsty, and we stopped for a much-needed cold drink in what we assumed was a restaurant in the lobby of our hotel. We placed our order, gulped down our drinks, and when the check was presented, my friend signed her name and room number. We got up and walked through the lobby to go up to our rooms, but nothing was familiar. We suddenly realized we weren't even in our hotel! We had a good laugh, went back and paid cash for the drinks, and we found our hotel just across the street.

The surroundings were similar to those with which we were familiar. However, we were deceived by subtle differences that caused us to make a mistake. Satan works much the same way to deceive us. At times we tend to rationalize our behavior because it seems harmless enough, until we are able to step back and realize we are trapped.

Another thing that tends to make us lose our way while trying to maintain a healthy perception about our bodies is fatigue. We are simply worn down in the struggle to resist all the false notions that are thrown at us. As my friend and I tried to find our way back to our hotel, we were tired. We had become hot and thirsty, and it was difficult to pay attention to where we really needed to be. We were then easily deceived. In the same way, on our paths to a healthier self-image, we need to stop once in a while to get our bearings, especially if the way is tedious and we get tired along the way. We may need to refocus, perhaps even in a different direction, until we can get back on course.

When we latch onto something that we can't or don't want to recognize as harmful, we sometimes feel certain that what we have in our grasp is worth holding onto. And, like the raccoon, we hang on for dear life. Even when we realize we are trapped, we are often unwilling to let go.

The world also entices us into thinking of the physical body as merely an object. Satan must be delighted to have so many voices inviting us to abuse or misuse this precious gift. Sister Susan Tanner, Young Women General President, has wisely taught, "[Satan] has filled the world with lies and deceptions about the body. He tempts many to defile this great gift of the body through unchastity, immodesty, self-indulgence, and addictions. He seduces some to despise their bodies; others he tempts to worship their bodies. In either case, he entices the world to regard the body merely as an object" ("The Sanctity of the Body," *Ensign*, Nov. 2005, 13).

These methods are just a few of the ways Satan uses to trap us. Various lifestyles and possessions are presented as must-haves. When we latch onto something that we can't or don't want to recognize as harmful, we sometimes feel certain that what we have in our grasp is worth holding onto. And, like the raccoon, we hang on for dear life. Even when we realize we are trapped, we are often unwilling to let go. What happens is most likely what we allow to happen. If we continue to cling, just as the raccoon does in the story, soon the consequences are beyond our control, perhaps even leading to our demise.

What is our first thought when we do get caught in one of Satan's snares? Can we see that we have, indeed, been trapped? Do we recognize that we are holding onto something to which we really don't want to be connected? Can we understand that we have been tricked into believing something that, although it has some truth to it, is harmful to us in the long run? Are we able to tell when our senses have become dulled to the point where we are deceived? Recognizing that we have been ensnared is the first step.

But, once we recognize that we have been trapped, we have a tendency to think that we are the victim. Victims are often perceived as helpless and not in control of the situation, and it's easy to feel pity or sorry for ourselves when we feel we are the victim. Seeking to be comforted or perhaps somewhat "in control," we are often tempted to turn to whatever it is that makes us feel better. In times of desperation or anxiety, where do we turn? Especially when we want to feel better *right now!* Do we surrender to addictive behavior? Do we go overboard in our eating habits? Do we depend on prescription drugs? Do we write physical or emotional checks that our bodies simply can't cash? On the flip side, maybe we spend *too* much time and effort sculpting our bodies. Are these addictive behaviors ways of trying to capture an artificial happiness that consistently eludes us?

Let me offer another perspective. When we find ourselves

in these kinds of predicaments, does it occur to us that we might need some repentance in our lives?

I wonder if anyone else has been guilty of thinking of "the other guy" when we hear a call to repentance. *Oh, I hope she's listening. This one's for her!* or *They're preaching to the choir. I don't need this.* Or how about, *This is a wicked world, alright. I'm sure glad I don't do the really bad stuff. That repentance thing is for all those sinful people out there who have those kinds of problems.*

> When we find ourselves in these kinds of predicaments, does it occur to us that we might need some repentance in our lives?

The LDS Bible Dictionary defines repentance as "a change of mind, i.e., a fresh view about God, and about oneself, and about the world. . . . a turning of the heart and will to God" (760). The word *sin* isn't even introduced until almost halfway through the lengthy definition!

As we turn our hearts and wills to God, we are then able to change the way we feel about ourselves, and we are on the road of repentance. Elder Russell M. Nelson gives us this assurance: "Uncontrolled appetite, addiction to pornography or harmful drugs, unbridled passion, carnal desire, and unrighteous pride are diminished with complete conversion to the Lord and a determination to serve Him and to emulate His example. Virtue garnishes their thoughts, and self-confidence grows" ("Repentance and Conversion," *Ensign*, May 2007, 104).

Certainly, as we become more in tune with our Heavenly Father, we come to understand what we need to do to change— on the outside as well as the inside. Repentance and having a change of heart will more fully enable us to make needed changes to our physical bodies. As we take care of our physical selves, we also take care of our mental and spiritual selves.

Change can happen, even one tiny step at a time.

Working toward a healthy weight can be a spiritually uplifting journey. I have learned the importance of true repentance—this change of mind and heart, and turning to God—as I have pleaded for His help in overcoming these earthly appetites and passions that seem to dominate so easily at times. I have often heard the same testimony from others in their quest. This form of repentance brings with it a better understanding of the intricate link between body, mind, and spirit.

We must be willing to let go of whatever started us on our road of self-destruction before we can move on. That can be much easier said than done. All of us have experienced the sorrow and grief that accompany the failure or malfunction of our physical bodies. Illness and suffering are, after all, the natural consequences of mortality. However, often, as a result of our lifestyles, we can also experience misery and despair. This regret, this unhappiness, can lead us in one of two directions. Our sorrow or regret can be extremely detrimental if we choose to give up and possibly sink deeper into the gaping, gloomy hole of hopelessness. However, it can also work for our good, if we strive for repentance and a

> *Working toward a healthy weight can be a spiritually uplifting journey. I have learned the importance of true repentance—this change of mind and heart, and turning to God—as I have pleaded for His help in overcoming these earthly appetites and passions that seem to dominate so easily at times.*

change of heart. Dr. Joan Borysenko stated, "Regret is a teacher—the key is to get its message and then let the messenger go" ("No Regrets," *Prevention* magazine, February 2005, 108).

I'm embarrassed to admit that for many years, I wondered if the Savior truly understood what I was feeling. This was not a thought I shared with anyone, yet it weighed heavily on my mind. I often did not feel "worthy," as there were times when I did not treat this physical body the way that I'm sure Heavenly Father intended for it to be treated. But for a long time, I wasn't convinced that He was really aware of the relationship that many of His children have with food. After all, "overeating" is not listed in the Topical Guide.

Our sorrow or regret can be extremely detrimental if we choose to give up and possibly sink deeper into the gaping, gloomy hole of hopelessness. However, it can also work for our good, if we strive for repentance and a change of heart.

And in considering the reason why many of us overeat, abuse drugs, even spend too much money or gamble, it is often because we find the challenges in our path insurmountable without a little help. We don't like what we are facing. We don't like the time and effort required to make needed changes. We want to feel better *right now*. Some things present themselves as easy answers and short-term solutions, but they can have long-term adverse consequences.

It was only when I really stopped to consider—digging deeper inside myself than I ever had before, studying the scriptures for keener insight than I ever had, spending more time in earnest prayer, and pouring out my heart as well as listening—that I was able to feel the calm reassurance that came quietly and peacefully.

I testify that He *does* know, that He *does* hear me, and that He most certainly *understands*. It was I who finally understood.

At a time in my life when I was really struggling with my own temptations, I delved into the scriptures and began to consider the powerful temptations Christ experienced as He was about to begin His earthly ministry. I found it almost unbelievable that the Lord fasted forty days in preparation, when I find it difficult to fast for even two meals.

One day, as I was studying further, a wonderful reassurance came to me as I was reading a passage that I had read many times before. In fact, one of the most peaceful, comforting feelings I have ever felt swept over me. I was studying the book of Luke. Jesus had just shared the feast of the Passover with His disciples and was now on the Mount of Olives, where he "kneeled down and prayed, saying, Father, if thou be willing, remove this cup from me: nevertheless not my will, but thine, be done" (Luke 22:41–42). Of course Jesus fulfilled the will of His Father. But there, for just an earthly moment, He too, experienced what it was like to not want to go forward with such an unimaginable trial. He, too, was hoping to have the cup removed. I read the passage again and again. Surely the Savior knows what it is to face a trial that seems dark, daunting, and impassible. He knows what it is like for us.

It made me think about the physical trials some of our

> *We don't like what we are facing. We don't like the time and effort required to make needed changes. We want to feel better right now. Some things present themselves as easy answers and short-term solutions, but they have long-term adverse consequences.*

children have gone through, and how that has affected my husband and me. What a strange sensation it was to want to stay pregnant forever when I knew that as soon as our twins were born, our daughter Emily's heart would soon stop beating. Aside from the pain of giving birth, I didn't want to go through that even more painful experience of losing her.

Surely the Savior knows what it is to face a trial that seems dark, daunting, and impassible. He knows what it is like for us.

I also remember well the trauma of delivering Eric, our tiny stillborn son. I didn't want to go through that, either.

Since writing my first book, I have become acquainted with many who have experienced heart-wrenching tragedies that I cannot even fathom. How difficult, even terrifying at times, it must be to go through such life-changing occurrences. Lives of good, faithful people are affected by illness, disease, an unfulfilled yearning for marriage, and the dashed hopes for children. I've communicated with those working to manage the chronic effects of physical and mental disabilities in loved ones, praying seemingly without success for children who, although remaining alive, seem lost forever through their own destructive choices. Others endure a temple marriage that ends in divorce, a lost job, a disability, a life damaged because of the cruel or unthinking actions of others. The pain often seems unbearable. Until we more fully understand, we find it so easy to want to turn to those immediate, worldly remedies for relief. It is especially at these times that we need to pause and be assured that our Savior understands how we feel, that He knows and cares about us.

What a bright spot in a world filled with sorrow and uncertainty, to understand the love and constancy that Jesus demonstrated in His atoning sacrifice and in carrying out the Father's will. It is assuring also to know that in the extremity of His suffering, "There appeared an angel unto him from heaven, strengthening him" (Luke 22:43). Though it may not be an angel that will comfort and sustain us, we can also receive divine strength in our personal struggles.

> *We find it so easy to want to turn to those immediate, worldly remedies for relief. It is especially at these times that we need to pause and be assured that our Savior understands how we feel, that He knows and cares about us.*

A sweet mother who had recently lost a baby sent me this message. The sadness of which she speaks could also result from facing other life tragedies: "As you well know, this has been the saddest time of my entire life. I never knew a body could cry so much. It has also been the most sanctifying experience. Through this profound loss, I have come to know the Savior's love for me in a very personal way. I greater appreciate Heavenly Father sacrificing His own, perfect Son. Ultimately, this experience has been just what I needed to help my husband and me progress spiritually in ways that could not have happened in any other way."

I have given this challenge to myself and know that I can accomplish it with heavenly help. And now I offer you the challenge. Is there something in your life that is powerfully attractive but that you know is harmful? Are you experiencing the kind of pain, stress, or discomfort where you are seeking other ways to feel some relief? Are those ways healthy or harmful? Will there be even more regret as you continue down the road you are currently on? Are you hanging on to something sparkly but harmful? Do you find yourself tightly wrapped around it? If so, stop what you're doing. Take a deep breath. Tell yourself it's going to be okay, that there are other, healthier ways of coping. Don't forget to spend some time on your knees and pray for strength as you seek to loosen your grip. Find some help. That's it. You can do it.

Now open your paw and let go!

Search and Rescue Tips

- Are there "glitzy" and "sparkly" harmful things in your life that you are holding onto? What do you need to empower you to let them go?
- What are you doing right now that will affect you long-term?
- Are you willing to think of the physical body as more than just an object? Our body houses our spirit. Ponder upon the intimate link between body, mind, and spirit.
- What do you need to do to turn your heart to God? Are there activities in your life you either need to stop engaging in or start engaging in to enjoy a complete conversion to the Lord?
- Just take one step at a time, and celebrate those steps that take you in the right direction. And enjoy the journey!

CHAPTER FOUR

Finding Nourishment

Some years ago, President Boyd K. Packer talked about a severe winter in Utah when the snow was excessive and had driven the deer herds down very low into some of the valleys. "Some of them were trapped by fences and circumstances as they were taken out of their natural habitat, and well-meaning, perfectly responsive, capable agencies tried to respond by feeding those deer to get them through the crisis of the winter. They brought in hay and dumped it everywhere; it was about as good as they could do under the circumstances. Later an immense number of those deer were found dead. The people who handled those animals afterward said that their stomachs were full of hay, but they had starved to death. They had been fed, but they had not been nourished" (as cited by Elder Jeffrey R. Holland in the Worldwide Leadership Training, February 10, 2007).

What are we permitting ourselves to be fed? Are we seeking

nourishment? That which we allow to enter our bodies greatly influences how those bodies respond—physically, mentally, and spiritually, which, in turn, can affect how we nurture others.

A dietician shared with me the difference between snacks and treats. Snacks, which are used to get us through until the next meal, should be on the nourishing side. Treats . . . well, they are just that. Treats. Although it's fine to have a little of both, it's important to keep in mind that treats simply feed. Healthy snacks can nourish and keep our bodies fueled. Like the deer in President Packer's example, our bodies need to be nourished, not just fed.

> *I believe that nourishing our bodies includes nurturing them. And when we truly nurture our bodies, we nurture our minds and spirits as well. I have discovered that the intimate connection between body, mind, and spirit is stronger than I had realized.*

I believe that nourishing our bodies includes *nurturing* them. And when we truly nurture our bodies, we nurture our minds and spirits as well. I have discovered that the intimate connection between body, mind, and spirit is stronger than I had realized. "When spirit and body are inseparably connected, they may receive a fulness of joy. But in this world, both body and spirit may be famished" (Truman Madsen, "The Savior, the Sacrament, and Self-Worth," *The Arms of His Love* [Salt Lake City: Bookcraft, 2000], 244).

Love is certainly an essential nutrient if we are to be nurtured, including love of self. But how easy is it to love ourselves?

When my daughter Hillary was seven years old, she wrote a poem entitled "I Love Me":

I Love Me!
I Love me so much!
I Take car[e] of me!
I Do everything
for me! I Just
Love Me!

When we are young, nurturing ourselves seems a lot less complicated. Our entire world consists of those who love and care for us. It is then that we form an opinion about our value. Recently I was visiting with a friend as she was holding her baby boy. I looked over at him, and I couldn't help but smile at his expression of absolute adoration for his mother. His tender smile for her was one of complete trust, unspeakable joy, and a sweet realization that she is his whole world.

Ah, wouldn't it be great if our children, as they get older, would continue to gaze at us the same way?

But as we mature, at some point in our lives, we begin to notice there are other ways to get approval and reinforcement. Even when we receive positive, loving messages at home, we continue to look to our expanding world for feedback and acceptance. That's all part of the plan. If we did not seek out others, we'd all still be living at home!

As we grow older, we sometimes become convinced that the world's view of what we ought to be is more important than what our parents might have taught us. Those counter voices come blaring at us from all sides. Ironically, they can also be powerful forces for good. Those with an opinion on what we ought to be include friends and those with whom we associate in the community, schools, and church. Visual images of the ideal body type and personality come to us daily through TV, the Internet, movies, popular magazines, newspapers, and books. As far as we allow these voices to sway us, they can exert tremendous influence as we continue to search for who we are and who we want to become.

Which voices are we heeding and allowing to influence us and our loved ones? There can be no doubt, these forces seek to shape our lives. What is their effect on us? Do we feel that happiness and acceptance will come only when we look a certain way, wear a certain size, or attain a certain level of prosperity or notoriety?

Do we feel that happiness and acceptance will come only when we look a certain way, wear a certain size, or attain a certain level of prosperity or notoriety?

Are we firmly anchored in the idea that the beauty within the divinely created bodies we have been given is sufficient? Or are we tempted to resort to radical make-overs of one kind or another?

Unfortunately, in today's climate, it is quite easy to allow ourselves to become "body critical." Unless we resist it, we can easily become overly judgmental of our own appearance. Some criticism can have a positive effect in helping us to see possibilities, but women tend to be hypercritical of themselves and others. In speaking to groups of women, I sometimes ask, "How many of you are happy with your body?" Over the years, I have encountered only a few raised hands. And, judging from written and spoken feedback, we all experience some degree of dissatisfaction. We can be critical of others, but we can be especially critical of ourselves. And the more we compare, the more critical we become. In a healthy dose, our concern over what others think of us is a natural inclination. But worrying excessively about the opinions of others can become a debilitating obsession.

Why do we feel the need to be so critical of ourselves? Especially when it brings such baggage as guilt, unhappiness, and discontent? Why do we insist on keeping it on board? Being too self-critical can easily turn into self-loathing. Self-loathing can increase as we compare ourselves to a standard—at times unrealistic—and we realize we just don't measure up. The self-loathing increases. Many of us feel that we don't deserve to experience happiness. We get to that unhappy place when we are too inwardly focused on our negative aspects.

Are we firmly anchored in the idea that the beauty within the divinely created bodies we have been given is sufficient? Or are we tempted to resort to radical makeovers of one kind or another?

I've found it useful to think of it this way: Would my Father in Heaven want me to loathe myself any more than I would want one of my own children to loathe himself or herself because he or she hasn't reached somebody else's notion of an ideal?

So what can we do? I have found that as we nourish our physical bodies, our desire to nurture our spirits will increase. And vice versa. As we seek nourishment for our spirits by filling our lives with that which we know is well worth our time and effort, we will be more inclined to nurture our physical bodies as well.

In a world where it is so easy to be critical of ourselves, what if we focused on, or at least were on the lookout for, our positive traits?

Take my friend Stacy. The other day, she propped her bare feet up on the coffee table. As she sat there, looking at her feet and wiggling her toes, she said, "Hey! My feet are pretty cute!"

That comment is so typical of Stacy. She has a contagiously positive and cheerful attitude—even when she faces challenges that aren't too positive or cheerful. After hearing about her cute feet, I came home and looked at my own. Hmmm. I would have to work pretty hard to be able to honestly say they were cute. Maybe a pedicure or even a little toenail polish would help, but at the moment, a thick pair of hiking socks to cover everything would help more.

> In a healthy dose, our concern over what others think of us is a natural inclination. But worrying excessively about the opinions of others can become a debilitating obsession.

Do you have cute feet? Okay, then, what about any other part of the amazing physical body with which you have so generously been blessed? Certainly when we enjoy and celebrate the positive, realizing we truly are "created after the image of God" (Mosiah 7:27), we can rejoice in the beauty of His greatest creation—all the way down to our toes!

When we look in the mirror, what do we see? One recent morning I studied my own appearance. I saw puffy eyes and more wrinkles than in an un-ironed blouse. Words such as *sad, pathetic,* and *dismal* came into my mind. I splashed a few handfuls of cool water on my tired morning face. I looked again in the mirror. I tried, with some difficulty, to change my view. As I gazed more intently, looking at the lines and rough spots, I finally remarked, "Pam, you have earned every one of those wrinkles!"

I didn't look any different, but I felt better.

Disney's Mulan looked in the mirror and wondered:

"Who is that girl I see, staring straight back at me?
Why is my reflection someone I don't know?
Somehow I cannot hide who I am, 'though I've tried.
When will my reflection show who I am inside?"
(Reflection, Disney's *Mulan*)

Sadly, I have heard from many women who, like Mulan, look in the mirror and wonder when their reflection will show who they are inside. And some have been looking and waiting for years. It is one of the most painfully difficult emotions to experience and to express—to recognize that the image is part of a self-made prison, and one that is terribly difficult to escape.

Christine, a newfound friend, gave me permission to include her heartfelt thoughts about her struggle: "I have felt like a complete failure. . . . I have been really suffering emotionally. I feel like a shell of the person I was. . . . We recently stayed at a hotel and there was a mirror on the wall at the foot of the bed, and I hated it because as I sat on the bed I had to stare at myself and I hated what I saw."

As we seek nourishment for our spirits by filling our lives with that which we know is well worth our time and effort, we will be more inclined to nurture our physical bodies as well.

I cried as I read her story of years of infertility, finally conceiving, only to lose the baby. "I was devastated and angry and did not feel like praying because I knew the Lord could have healed that little baby if He had wanted to. . . . I turned to the Lord to strengthen my faith that He had my best interest in mind, and I promised Him that if I were to face more trials I

> "I was devastated and angry and did not feel like praying because I knew the Lord could have healed that little baby if He had wanted to. . . . I turned to the Lord to strengthen my faith that He had my best interest in mind, and I promised Him that if I were to face more trials I would turn to Him instead of trying to deal with them myself and that I would not become bitter."

would turn to Him instead of trying to deal with them myself and that I would not become bitter."

Over the next few years, this sweet woman endured even more heartache. At last becoming pregnant once more, she carried twins, but they survived just a few hours. I understood her poignant comment, "My heart broke, and I cried a cry I had never before heard or felt."

And, interestingly enough, in reading comments from around the world, I have found that women—and men—no matter what their status, experience this taxing sensation, even when the world judges them to be "pleasing," or "acceptable."

For example, Kaley wrote, "So many times people told me I was pretty, and I wouldn't let myself believe them because I felt so ugly. I then thought of them (in my mind) as liars and had a hard time trusting people. . . . [However, I've since] found trust in people, and I have found that God really does love me. I now love myself, and realize it's okay if other people love me."

What an honest, insightful response. I love to read letters from people. I especially enjoy reading about the increased understanding that comes when an individual is able to feel nurtured and to see the reflection our Father in Heaven wants us to see.

Truman Madsen has said, "The Lord gives us glimpses of ourselves. And in self-examination we are most blessed when we see ourselves as we are seen by him and know ourselves as we are known by him, then, knowledge of the Savior and self-knowledge increase together. In this world, we do not really grasp who we are until we know whose we are" ("The Savior, the Sacrament, and Self-Worth," *The Arms of His Love* [Salt Lake City: Deseret Book, 2000], 246).

> *I soon discovered that taking a walk, even a brief walk, was physically, emotionally, and yes, spiritually nurturing and uplifting—even lifesaving.*

Grasping and holding onto that concept is sometimes a slippery process. Many of us, while on a quest for knowledge of who we are, do so while possessing physical bodies that are not what we would have particularly hoped for in this life. Sometimes we struggle to appreciate these bodies when all we can see are the defects.

As I wrote in *Running with Angels*, I began walking on a regular basis after the death of our second baby. I felt hopeless despair after his little lifeless body was born. I started walking not as a means of weight loss, although I had more than 100 pounds to lose, but simply because I wanted to feel better. I soon discovered that taking a walk, even a brief walk, was physically, emotionally, and yes, spiritually nurturing and uplifting—even lifesaving. Those walks included silent prayers, and listening— real listening—as I yearned to be nurtured by my Father in Heaven and to understand what it was He wanted me to learn in going through these earthly ordeals.

53

Since then I have encountered numerous additional bumps in the road. There will always be cracks and even huge potholes in all of our paths. But I am amazed at the resiliency of the human spirit as well as of the human body. I have met people who display such resiliency. They experience difficulties but are eager to raise the bar on their commitment level and gain a respect for their body instead of hating it.

Sonja wrote a poignant personal account:

I too have suffered through the loss of miscarriages and two stillborn sons. . . . My dear husband faithfully filled each of my prescriptions for pain that automatically came home with me from the hospital after each loss. I never took any of them until after the death of our fourth baby. I had an ample supply and quickly found myself self-medicating to "numb up." I soon started adding alcohol to the mix (I SOOOO knew better than that!), and I developed a liking [for] my new zombie way of life. It was as if I was hiding from the pain and from the world. I felt like I got "Poor Sonja" looks from everyone I saw. I hated feeling pitied. I lived in flannel pajama pants and carried around a blanket. I would go from lying on my bed to sitting in the recliner, wrapped up in my blanket, staring out the window at nothing. I only went out when I had to. I simply existed. When I took the painkiller, I would just be in a haze, and it felt comfortable. Like my pajama pants and my blanket. I don't remember what my kids were doing, I don't think I cared. I do remember being angry with them, and resenting them because they needed me, and I had nothing to give. I was so empty, so tired, so void of emotion. Wow. As I write, I realize that I still have a lot of guilt about this. When I wasn't in a medication-induced haze, I hurt so much. I felt so much guilt. I blamed myself. After three losses, I felt like I had no business getting pregnant again. I should have known what the outcome would be with another pregnancy, yet I let myself hope for that "rainbow baby." After my last loss, I said horrible, hateful things to myself every day. The intense feelings of self-hatred were so uncomfortable. So I hid from them by self-medicating. Even though I knew I shouldn't.

Then, when I ran out of the painkiller, I even considered stealing it from various sources, although I never went that far. I finally sought help from a very wise and loving bishop. He helped me to see that I was headed down a road that I didn't want to go down. He helped me to see that I was being self-destructive. He told me something that I will never forget. He said, "It is okay to hurt. Let yourself feel the feelings. If you feel angry, be angry. If you are angry at Heavenly Father, tell him! If you need to cry, cry." He gave me permission to grieve. Giving me that permission was something I couldn't do for myself. When I told him that it was too hard, he looked at me and said, "Sonja, you can do hard things! I have seen you. You can do hard

> *"I finally sought help from a very wise and loving bishop. He helped me to see that I was headed down a road that I didn't want to go down. He helped me to see that I was being self-destructive."*

things." So many times I played this over and over in my head. I have so much love and respect for my bishop. He is another one of those blessings that Heavenly Father gave to me. He and my husband gave me several priesthood blessings during this time. Those also played a big role in my healing.

Although I was healing, my eating habits were horrible. The pain was pretty intense. I found myself turning to food for comfort. During the low time, as I hated my body because I felt like it was responsible for killing my babies, I wanted to punish it. So the gas station/convenience store just down the street became my new friend. I never walked the two blocks to get to it, I always drove! As soon as I got my son off to school, I would go there for my morning 32 oz. Dr. Pepper, usually accompanied by a pack of peanut M&Ms. I would go again for lunch and refill my 32 oz. cup, often accompanied only by chips. Dinner was usually another 32 oz. refill and whatever else I could find. I never went to bed hungry. I always had ice cream, cookies, butter-lovers popcorn or whatever else I could scrounge up. My pantry and freezer were full of convenience foods: frozen pizzas, anything microwavable or processed. I

> *"Eating was another way that I self-medicated. It was comfort to me. It did make me feel guilty, but feeling guilty about food was so much easier to take than feeling guilty about my babies, or feeling guilty about not taking care of my family, or feeling guilty about my poor choices."*

didn't ever cook well-balanced meals for my family. Eating was another way that I self-medicated. It was comfort to me. It did make me feel guilty, but feeling guilty about food was so much easier to take than feeling guilty about my babies, or feeling guilty about not taking care of my family, or feeling guilty about my poor choices.

I e-mailed you after I had finished *Running with Angels* the first time. Reading it planted a seed. I knew that I wanted to be free of the burden of grief that I was hauling around with me all of the time. I knew that I wanted to take control of my life and be the person I should be. I knew I wanted to eat better and take care of myself, but it took me several months to finally decide to do something about it. Holding onto the pain was the only way I knew to keep my babies' memory alive. I was worried that if I let it go, I would let them go.

General conference in spring 2006 was the turning point. I was still so weighed down with my "garbage bag" full of negative emotions—guilt, anger, self-loathing, etc. The Sunday afternoon session was just starting. My two younger kids had fallen asleep, and my oldest was playing with Legos while we watched conference. I told my husband that I was going for a walk. I put my headphones on and listened to conference while I walked. I walked to the cemetery where my boys are buried and laid on the grass next to them. Joseph B. Wirthlin gave an amazing talk on living an abundant life. I decided that I wanted an abundant life. I sat at the cemetery for a long time. I prayed, I talked to my boys. I visualized myself handing my garbage bag over to the Savior.

I didn't want to carry it around with me anymore, I couldn't carry it anymore. I know it sounds simple, but I left the cemetery a changed person. I felt an emotional change, as well as a physical change. I felt strengthened and renewed. I knew that the Savior had taken that burden for me.

After that, I read *Running with Angels* again. It lit the fire in me, and I started running. ME— running! It was so hard at first, but I knew I could do hard things. My bishop told me I could. As I started making better choices, I started feeling better and better. I remember waking up one day and laughing because I felt so happy, so free.

I have recently come to the realization that my living children need me to be the mom that they deserve, my husband needs me to be the wife I want to be, and I am, and always have been, worthy of living a more healthy life by eating more nutritious food and exercising regularly. . . . I am a daughter of God; I am a mother of angels, on earth and in heaven, who will

"After that, I read Running with Angels *again. It lit the fire in me, and I started running. ME—running! It was so hard at first, but I knew I could do hard things. My bishop told me I could. As I started making better choices, I started feeling better and better. I remember waking up one day and laughing because I felt so happy, so free."*

always be part of me. Those are not small things. I owe it to them *and* to me to take care of me. Sharing my story and being there for other women in pain has also helped me to heal.

I met Sonja and had some additional interaction with her before I realized it was she who had written me her story a year or so earlier. I would never have been able to tell from simply talking to her that she had experienced all she had. What drew me to her e-mail in the first place was the ache she felt upon losing her children. It was all too familiar. When something is so painful, we are willing to do almost anything to feel better, *even when we know better.* Often it takes angelic nurturing from someone in our earthly lives to help us to see the light at the end of the tunnel.

> *When something is so painful, we are willing to do almost anything to feel better,* even when we *know better. Often it takes angelic nurturing from someone in our earthly lives to help us to see the light at the end of the tunnel.*

As she was able to make the positive change, Sonja even went on to train for and run a marathon. About that experience, she wrote, "During long runs, when I would be so tired and would want to quit, I remembered what my bishop told me, and I would chant, 'I can do hard things. I am a marathoner.' That became part of my 'marathon mantra.'"

Sonja is now sharing her strength and experience through many kind acts of service. Her body and spirit were quite forgiving when she made an abrupt halt on her road to self-destruction. She realized that her Heavenly Father loved her all along. She was able to experience a miracle as she began nurturing her body—and her spirit.

The human mind and body are truly a miracle. President Gordon B. Hinckley expressed the wonder of it in this way: "Have you ever contemplated the wonders of yourself, the eyes with which you see, the ears with which you hear, the voice with which you speak? No camera ever built can compare with the human eye. No method of communication ever devised can compare with the voice and the ear. No pump ever built will run as long or as efficiently as the human heart. No computer or other creation of science can equal the human brain. What a remarkable thing you are. You can think by day and dream by night. You can speak and hear and smell. Look at your finger. The most skillful attempt to reproduce it mechanically has resulted in only a crude approximation. The next time you use your finger, watch it, look at it, and sense the wonder of it. . . . You are a child of God, His crowning creation" ("The Body Is Sacred," *New Era*, Nov. 2006, 2).

> *The human body is a sacred miraculous creation! It is an extraordinary gift, one to be received with gratitude and treated with honor and respect, even reverence.*

Recently, I visited an exhibit about the human body. I was overwhelmed by the cadavers that had been extraordinarily preserved, showing the complexity of the human body. How marvelous we are! Each of the various body functions was identified, including respiratory, circulatory, muscular, skeletal, nervous, digestive, and reproductive. It was humbling to see each complex fiber of veins, arteries, bronchial tubes, and the tiny bones and fibers that make up each little part of our bodies. The human body is a sacred miraculous creation! It is an extraordinary gift, one to be received with gratitude and treated with honor and respect, even reverence. After viewing that display, I understood more clearly why Paul would write: "Know ye not that ye are the temple of God, and that the Spirit of God dwelleth in you?" (1 Corinthians 3:16).

One of the ways we can honor our bodies is to observe the Word of Wisdom. President Ezra Taft Benson taught, "The condition of the physical body can affect the spirit. That's why the Lord gave us the Word of Wisdom. He also said that we should retire to our beds early and arise early (see D&C 88:124), that we should not run faster than we have strength (see D&C 10:4; Mosiah 4:27), and that we should use moderation in all good things. . . . Food can affect the mind, and deficiencies in certain elements in the body can promote mental depression. . . . Rest and physical exercise are essential, and a walk in the fresh air can refresh the spirit. Wholesome recreation is part of our religion, and a change of pace is necessary, and even its anticipation can lift the spirit. . . . Healthful food, proper rest, adequate exercise, and a clear conscience can prepare us to tackle the trials that lie ahead" (*The Teachings of Ezra Taft Benson* [Salt Lake City: Bookcraft, 1988, 475–76).

I love the promise associated with the keeping of the Word of Wisdom: "And all saints who remember to keep and do these sayings, walking in obedience to the commandments, shall receive health in their navel and marrow to their bones; and shall find wisdom and great treasures of knowledge, even hidden treasures; and shall run and not be weary, and shall walk, and not faint" (D&C 89:18–20).

I love the promise associated with the keeping of the Word of Wisdom: "And all saints who remember to keep and do these sayings, walking in obedience to the commandments, shall receive health in their navel and marrow to their bones; and shall find wisdom and great treasures of knowledge, even hidden treasures; and shall run and not be weary, and shall walk, and not faint" (D&C 89:18–20).

I recall with fondness those who helped me make it through my first marathon. In turn, I felt happy to help someone else. And someday, I'm sure she will enlighten and encourage others through a life marathon of their own.

Thinking about running and not being weary reminds me of my third marathon. I'd had some injuries, and that year I couldn't seem to set aside the needed training time. So I decided, with my marathon buddies, Ruth and Dianne, to run/walk the St. George Marathon. That year we had a specific purpose. We decided to be "Team Thomas," with matching blue T-shirts and all. Thomas is Dianne's teenage son, who is battling leukemia. He is like his mother—positive, happy, and hopeful. Dianne is my dear friend, who, during my second marathon, also at St. George, decided that the only part of her body that didn't ache by about Mile 19 (out of 26.2) was her earlobes. She was full of jokes and cheerful stories when we needed a pick-me-up.

During that grueling but actually quite enjoyable day, I thought about Thomas. He has already experienced more in his young life than we can comprehend, and yet he has spread more sunshine and inspiration than perhaps he realizes. And that day, I learned a lesson in nurturing that I had not even anticipated.

That lesson has to do with the cyclical nature of nurturing. While running and walking the course, Dianne, Ruth, and I visited with each other as well as others along the way. Although we knew it would be our "longest participation time" on the marathon course, we had just as much fun. Well, actually, Ruth preferred running the whole way so as to not prolong the agony. But wasn't she sweet to hang back with us? What a good sport. Ruth was the one who convinced me years ago that I could even run a marathon. My desire was there, all right, but she and Dianne were so encouraging. What wonderful friends.

We chatted, grabbed cups of water, and paused for blister checks through the first sixteen or so miles. Then I thought it would be nice to allow my experienced running buddies to go on ahead of me those last eight miles. (Okay. I'll admit it. I would have loved to have kept up with them.)

From about Mile 10, a young woman began running next to us. As we talked off and on, she shared with me her fear of not being able to finish this, her first marathon. She was recently married, and her new husband and other family members were up ahead of her. After Ruth and Dianne had moved on, she and I stayed together. Even through my own self-inflicted pain and discomfort, I felt myself encouraging her, pausing for side-ache-stops, and visiting with her about almost everything under the scorching Utah sun to get her mind (and mine as well) off our prolonged struggle. She shared much of her life with me, including her dreams and concerns, even reaching beyond the marathon. By the time we got to Mile 24, she felt much better. She knew she could do those last two miles on her own, and I smiled, or at least tried to smile, as she left me in the hot red dust.

I was thrilled to see that the other members of Team

Thomas were waiting for me, their "sweeper," to welcome me across the finish line with a Popsicle and a smile.

I learned much that day. Out of our love and regard for a young man and his family, I learned how indomitable our bodies and spirits can be. Thomas's young body has been through a lengthy, intense workout from the leukemia, yet he continues to fight. I see his positive outlook, as well as that of his sweet mother. I am also privileged to witness the unending nurturing she and her husband provide their son. It inspires me to continue to fight my own battles and to nurture this body I have been given, as well as nurture my family.

> As we nurture others, we can feel nurtured ourselves. Then the cycle begins again. The boost we get from feeling nurtured enables us to again nurture those around us. What a wonderful, recurring concept!

I also learned something valuable from the experience I had with the young woman during the marathon. I had not met her before that day. I have not seen her since, nor may I ever see her again. However, we shared something positive that I will remember forever. I recall with fondness those who helped me make it through my first marathon. In turn, I felt happy to help someone else. And someday, I'm sure she will enlighten and encourage others through a life marathon of their own.

I had spent more time nurturing that day than I ever imagined, but I was also much more nurtured than I ever anticipated. As we nurture others, we can feel nurtured ourselves. Then the cycle begins again. The boost we get from feeling nurtured enables us to again nurture those around us. What a wonderful, recurring concept!

And as we continue nourishing, not just feeding, we will discover greater self-love and self-acceptance. We will become less critical of ourselves. We will be able to more fully focus on the positive, and the reflection we see of ourselves will be truer to what the Lord sees and *intends for us to see!*

Search and Rescue Tips

- Ask: Are we simply feeding ourselves? Or are we taking the time and effort to truly nurture our bodies and our spirits?
- Take a walk, or incorporate some other activity into your life. It can be physically, emotionally, and spiritually nurturing— even lifesaving!
- Criticism, in a healthy dose, *can* have a positive effect. Being overly critical can have a very negative effect.
- In what ways can we more fully observe the Word of Wisdom?
- Ask: Are we nurturing ourselves as we reach out to nurture others? Do we allow others to nurture us?

CHAPTER FIVE

Finding Power in Positive Examples

The morning began like many other soccer days—gray and cold. We got to the field just as the skies opened up to chilly wet rain. Near the field was an area of construction where I could see the precipitation wearing down the soil, washing it away. What a mess. I was happy we could find a parking space just behind our son, playing keeper, guarding his team's goal. It was unusual, but because of the construction, the spectators were able to park right next to the field. I knew I needed to be quiet and a bit incognito as I sat there in the nice, dry car. Taking his umbrella, Mark went to sit on the sidelines with the other spectators who had come to watch our team play.

I rolled the window down just enough to hear the action. Because of where I was sitting and not having anybody to talk to except myself, I could easily hear the players as well as the parents on both sides. What I heard that morning was quite revealing.

Family members of our boys were relatively quiet. There was an occasional "Good Job!" or "C'mon, ref!" The parents and fans of the opposing team, however, were much more vocal. Instead of positive comments, though, I heard negative, nasty ones; not only hurled at the referees but also to our players and even their own team members. Demeaning comments. I've been to countless games and have heard many such comments flung onto the field. However, I could easily see that day how these especially hurtful remarks drew shameful attention to the boys and their efforts, not to mention to the parents themselves.

The negative comments were unrelenting. By the second half, although the score was tied, our boys were crushed. They didn't play with nearly the enthusiasm that they had at the beginning of the game. By now, parents on both sides were yelling at the other side to be quiet. It wasn't pretty. The other team fed off of their parents' hostility, and our boys got riled up as well. Penalty cards were handed out right and left. The referee had to stop the game to calm everyone down, which he should have done much earlier in the game. It was difficult to watch such talented players on both sides be so negatively affected by behavior of the parents. By the time it was over, both teams seemed to have lost heart.

That day I watched a powerful concept in action. We may not fully realize it, but our remarks and our actions have a tremendous influence on not only our children but other children as well. Granted, they were playing ball, and tough things are often said to kids playing ball. However, I'd never heard such a barrage of hurtful, unnecessary comments. They affected the players on both sides, wearing them down, little by little, just as the falling rain wore away the soil. After a while, there wasn't much of a good feeling left, anywhere on the field.

What about our attitudes and values in other areas of our lives that we model to children? Often we don't realize how closely they watch us and mirror our actions and words.

I had a bit of a wake-up call years ago. In the middle of the day, I knelt down by the side of my bed to pray. I had closed my bedroom door but had not locked it. It wasn't long before I heard the door open softly and felt the eyes of then four-year-old Stephen watching me. I sensed his surveillance for quite some time. Then he whispered, "Mom, what are you doing?"

I couldn't help but smile. Apparently my son did not often see me in personal prayer. Okay, he rarely saw me. And it must have been *quite* rare, since he wasn't sure what to make of it. Wouldn't it be nice for him—for all of my children—to at least once in a while notice me turning to the Lord? Certainly they catch me when I *don't* want them noticing what I do.

Unfortunately, it goes without saying, that our not-so-divine qualities and examples get noticed, too.

I have this shoe box where I keep a little stash of chocolate. I really don't keep it full, but once in a while it's nice to get a little nibble. As I went one recent day to "the box," I noticed a little trail of wrappers on the floor, leading away from the supposedly secret treasure. They had been dropped by a chocolate-thief, obviously not very careful about hiding the evidence. I soon discovered chocolaty confirmation on the mouths of a few children. I have since told them to not even bother trying to find the new hiding place.

Although it's okay to have a treat once in a while, I have also worked hard to be a more effective role model as I have discovered and tried to live a healthier lifestyle. The change in my example has really hit home for me as I have expressed to my children in words as well as actions my enjoyment of running.

They have supported me in events as they have cheered me across the finish line. They have helped in putting on the Running with Angels 5K benefit event. And they also love to run. I enjoy watching them get fulfillment out of something I have enjoyed as well.

Women have a unique way of influencing children, and that which is important to us will certainly become apparent to the children in our lives. I recall with fondness the music that permeated our home as I was growing up. My mother would often sing as she worked and went about her day. I think she would have made a fine star on Broadway, had she not stopped to raise her family! A love of music is one of the greatest legacies my mother gave to her children. She took us to symphonies, and Mr. Peterson painstakingly taught us how to play the piano week after week. I felt my mother's passion for music as I grew up. I remember the night she and my dad took me to an opera (although, my dad listened through an earpiece to the second half of a University of Utah basketball game). She loves the performing arts and has passed that love on to me. I thoroughly enjoy listening to Vivaldi. John Denver, Johann Sebastian Bach, and Celine Dion are right up there, too. I will be eternally grateful for the love of all music that my mother helped to nurture in me.

> *Women have a unique way of influencing children, and that which is important to us will certainly become apparent to the children in our lives.*

And while I'm talking about the power of my sweet mother's example, as I get close to the age myself of having grandchildren, I realize that when our twins, Amy and Emily were born, it was not only difficult for Mom to see little Emily die, it was also hard

70

on her to see her own daughter go through such heartache. A double whammy. She has always set such an example of love and strength. I love the poem she wrote at that time.

OUR EMILY
Carolee L. Harmon

This day-old child who just arrived
with tiny mouth and hands
Will soon be going home again
obeying divine commands.
But wait . . . we have so many plans for her
it really seems unfair.
Bedtime stories and nursery rhymes
and secrets sweet to share.
Valentines and cookies to make,
cousins for her to know.
We want to buy her dolls and books
and watch her talents grow.
She needs to feel the seasons change,
giggle with friends among.
Blow candles out on frosted cakes
when "Happy Birthday" is sung!
We want to teach her things of Thee
with loving, kind concern
And sing our favorite Primary songs
So much for her to learn!
But wiser, she, than all of us
wrinkles her little nose
As if to say: "He needs me more
than you do, I suppose . . .
So I'll go back to Heavenly Father,

my mission here is done
But He'll let Amy fill your hearts
with twice the joy and fun.
I came to gain a body,
claim these parents for my own
We're now a family unit
so I'll never be alone.
Such happiness! To know I'm loved
and fulfilled my part with birth.
You have to live with much more faith
to stay here on the earth.
This day I spent with you's enough . . .
My dad gave me a blessing
The hardest part is leaving
Mommy's arms, I am confessing . . ."
Then she was gone. But this thought dwells:
What she brought, none can sever
And if we do our part—we'll be
A family forever!

As we get older, we more fully realize the examples our parents and other nurturers have set for us. However, we may never entirely realize the example we have set for the children in our lives. Often we won't see it until they grow up, go out into the world, and mirror what we have taught them and the way in which we have lived. But often we can see right away how our attitudes and values affect our children, such as their display of sportsmanship, their love of reading and writing, their desire to offer their own personal prayers, or even their aspirations to lace up their running shoes and go for a run.

Of particular importance is the view and attitude we have toward our own bodies. Elder Jeffrey R. Holland has wisely taught: "If you are obsessing over being a size 2, you won't be very surprised when your daughter or the Mia Maid in your class does the same and makes herself physically ill trying to accomplish it" (*Modesty, Makeovers, and the Pursuit of Physical Beauty* [Salt Lake City: Deseret Book Co., 2006], 18).

We adult women are tremendous examples and resources for young women. Conveying healthy attitudes about our bodies will be more effectively taught through our actions. How can we go about it?

The answer varies with each young woman. Hopefully we know our own daughters best and can enjoy open communication with them from early in their lives. As I thought more about this, I decided to visit with some young women about what they felt that we as mothers could do to help convey to our daughters healthy attitudes about themselves. One of the first comments I heard from these 17- and 18-year-olds was about the "huge impact" mothers have on their daughters. Enjoying a closeness with their mother is a huge factor in helping these young women feel more secure. They observed that "when mothers are confident, their daughters are more likely to be confident." Mothers, they also said, should encourage daughters to be "healthy" rather than "thin." One young woman said she thought mothers should focus on "other stuff, like a sense of humor, rather than looks."

The influence we have as women can be profound. I

> *We may never entirely realize the example we have set for the children in our lives. Often we won't see it until they grow up, go out into the world, and mirror what we have taught them and the way in which we have lived.*

recently spoke to a friend with young children and whose own mother was having some lifting and tucking done through plastic surgery. She told me how confusing that was to her young daughters when they discovered during Grandma's recovery why she had bruises and wasn't feeling well. We are bombarded with worldly messages that tell us our looks are what matters. "'If your looks are good enough, your life will be glamorous and you will be happy and popular.' That kind of pressure is immense in the teenage years, to say nothing of later womanhood. In too many cases too much is being done to the human body to meet just such a fictional (to say nothing of superficial) standard" (ibid., 19).

Trying to set a good example for her overweight daughter, one woman wrote: "I want desperately to help my daughter lose this weight and find the happiness I know she could have. I just don't know how to help her. . . . I love her so much my heart aches. I can't stand to see what this weight is doing to her life." I think one of the best things that this mother can do is to continue to love her daughter and be supportive of any positive effort she makes about improving her lifestyle, without criticizing. Her daughter needs to be the one to seek out that "push" she needs. No

> The influence we have as women can be profound. I recently spoke to a friend with young children and whose own mother was having some lifting and tucking done through plastic surgery. She told me how confusing that was to her young daughters when they discovered during Grandma's recovery why she had bruises and wasn't feeling well.

one wants to get a shove when they are not ready for it. Hopefully, it will click for her daughter, and both women will be grateful for the unconditional love and encouragement that will have always been there.

A mother's influence takes effect very early. One of the first things we do upon coming into the world as infants is to reflect on our surroundings. Funny faces are made at us, and we respond by smiling, giggling, or mimicking what we see. Studies have shown how babies respond to their mother's voice, face, and even smell. They look to their mother for protection, guidance, and direction. As they grow into little girls, they may watch their mothers and older sisters dressing up and wander into their closets to try on their dresses and high heels. Hillary absolutely loves the makeup drawers of her older sisters, much to their chagrin, as they come home to broken lipsticks and divots taken out of eye shadow. Hillary is not alone. Younger siblings desperately seek to look like the older women in their lives. The mirrors are all around them.

As I've watched my own children growing up, I can see how early on they trust their mother's judgment of what they wear, how she combs their hair (which I admit has been terrifying at times), what they watch on television, and even their playmates. The time eventually comes where they take control of just which shirt they'll wear with which pants and with whom they will associate after school. For those first precious years, their father and I were the ones they trusted to give them feedback about their world. As they continue to grow older, experiencing more of the world around them, they also process comments and reactions of others. Hopefully we will have effectively taught them about their value, and they will have learned, so that on the way through their worldly experience and back to their eternal home they will be able to hear heavenly voices a little more loudly than those from the world around them.

A sweet Primary girl named Megan heard heavenly voices when she was young and came back to them as she grew older. She was in our ward and would come over to play with Nicholas when he was a little boy. He loved to see her come, especially during the time I was on bed rest during my pregnancy with Amy and Emily, which must have seemed like an eternity to him. Megan remembers when the twins were born. She turned eleven on the day Emily died. Now a grown woman, here is part of the letter she recently shared:

Hopefully we will have effectively taught them about their value, and they will have learned, so that on the way through their worldly experience and back to their eternal home they will be able to hear heavenly voices a little more loudly than those from the world around them.

"I sang with the other Primary children at Emily's funeral. While singing the song 'I Lived in Heaven,' is the first time I can remember feeling the Spirit so strong and knowing how real God is in our lives and *knowing* where I was going after this life and *believing* it with my whole heart. I remember her little pretty casket. That day was the day my *own* testimony was first planted.

"I was a Primary chorister for five years. Whenever I taught that song, I would share that story with the children. I would tell them how I felt at the funeral. And each time we would sing that song, I would tell them to sing for baby Emily, and they would belt that song out with their whole

76

hearts. I think my testimony from that song helped them develop their own testimony of the next life."

How inspiring it is to see how Megan was affected and how she has gone on to motivate others with their own testimonies!

Hopefully each of us is part of the throng of heavenly voices, offering strength and reassurance. Constructive criticism has its place. We also need positive support and encouragement in our quest to discover more about ourselves and our earthly and eternal roles. We can have a huge impact on the children (as well as the adults!) in our lives. They are important. They do matter, and their efforts can be worthwhile. And *that* concept comes across much more effectively if we believe it ourselves.

Search and Rescue Tips

- Think about messages we are sending through our comments and attitudes. What examples can be seen in our reflection?
- Think about the positive examples you have seen in your own life. What can you learn from them?
- How do our children view us as we view our own bodies? Are we happy with that view? Or at least content? Do we obsess about looking better?
- Do we show a healthy attitude about living a healthy life?
- We may never know how our lives will inspire others, who will, in turn, inspire those with whom they interact. Take a child to the symphony!

CHAPTER SIX

Finding Inner Strength through Perseverance

Whew! The 2007 New Year's Day Fiesta Bowl was quite a game! My husband, Mark, from a small farming community in southeastern Idaho, described the football matchup between Boise State and the University of Oklahoma as "the farm boys of Idaho against the big shots from the city." As I am from the "big city" of Salt Lake, we've done some friendly teasing back and forth over the years about small towns versus big cities (although I think one of the brothers-in-law really means what he says). The University of Oklahoma is located in Norman, just outside Oklahoma City and has 10,000 more students than does Boise State (Wikipedia, internet info).

For much of the game, I was just as entertained watching Mark watch his "good ole Idaho boys 'winning' the big city boys," especially since the Oklahoma Sooners were favored to beat the Boise Broncos by 7½ points. The game was exciting. Near the end of the fourth quarter, Jared Zabransky, the Boise

State quarterback, threw an interception that led to a touch-down by Oklahoma. There was just one minute and six seconds left in the game. *Ouch,* I thought, *that is gonna be one long walk back to the locker room after this loss.* However, after some miraculous plays, the score was tied as time ran out.

During overtime, more incredible plays were executed. Oklahoma played a great game. But Boise State went on to win, 43 to 42. When he was inter-viewed after the game, Zabransky said: "It would have been easy to give up on us with a minute left, but we had a lot of magic left." He knew the game wasn't over until the time on the score-board read 00:00. It certainly would have been easy for him to hang his head and quit after throwing an interception so close to the end of the game. But he and his teammates continued to try. Had they lost heart and quit fighting, there would have been a different outcome.

Perseverance, in the right direction, reveals inner strength. And inner strength can lead to more confidence about our physical bodies, including a more positive self-image.

In pulling off the improbable, the Boise State Broncos perse-vered. They believed in themselves and reached down deep for the inner strength they needed to combine with their physical strength to realize their dream.

Even those who are not sports fans can learn a lesson from this example. Perseverance, in the right direction, reveals inner strength. And inner strength can lead to more confidence about our physical bodies, including a more positive self-image.

Often, when I am sweating on the elliptical machine or siz-ing up the hill ahead of me on my morning walk, I ask myself, *How badly do I want this?* Ooooh, I've asked myself that over and over, and over, especially in the never-ending quest of trying to achieve or maintain a healthy weight. When I persevere, I feel greater inner strength. And when I feel greater inner strength, I also enjoy a more robust sense of self-esteem, which has been described by Dr. Steven Hawks as "a sense of joy that is experienced when inherent potential is discovered and realized" (*Making Peace with the Image in the Mirror* [Salt Lake City: Bookcraft, 2001], 97).

President James E. Faust described self-esteem as "what we think of ourselves, how we relate to what others think of us, and the value of what we accomplish." Notice he didn't write "what others think of us," rather "how we relate to what others think of us." The self-esteem that President Faust talks about "is not blind, arrogant, vain, self-love but rather a self-esteem that is self-respecting, honest, and without conceit. It is born of inner peace and strength." What a beautiful and inspiring description!

President Faust went on to say, "Self-esteem goes to the very heart of our personal growth and accomplishment. It is the glue that holds together our self-reliance, our self-control, our self-approval or disapproval and keeps all self-defense mechanisms secure. It is a protection against excessive self-deception, self-distrust, self-reproach, and plain old-fashioned selfishness" ("The Value of Self-Esteem," CES Fireside for Young Adults, May 6, 2007).

On the eve of running my second marathon, while I was trying to rev up my self-esteem, I was grateful to receive a nice note from Adria, one of the sweet young women in our ward. In her short message, she wrote, "Good Luck!! I have been studying ancient Greece in school, and just the other day we heard about the Battle of Marathon. Following Greece's victory, the very first marathon was run. Unfortunately, the runner wasn't prepared, and died. Good Luck! I know you'll do awesome."

I thought about Adria's note at various times the next day during the 26.2-mile ordeal. Especially around Mile 18, when I was *sure* I wasn't prepared, and I felt my inner resolve weakening. I seriously wondered if I would suffer the same fate as did that first marathoner. However, I also realized that poor guy didn't have anyone handing him water, fruit, Band-Aids, and ibuprofen. He was probably wearing sandals or perhaps no shoes at all. And certainly there were no brightly colored posters saying, "Way to go! Only 21 more miles!!" and "What do you need toenails for, anyway?"

> *Sometimes others say things about us or to us that aren't so nice. Their words and actions can hurt. As hard as it is to do, we mustn't let those comments make us self-conscious.*

Thinking about Adria's sweet note helped me to persevere to the finish line.

However, sometimes others say things about us or to us that aren't so nice. Their words and actions can hurt. As hard as it is to do, we mustn't let those comments make us self-conscious. In a talk given to young women, Elder Jeffrey R. Holland counseled: "Please be more accepting of yourselves, including your body shape and style, with a little less longing to look like someone else. We are all different. Some are tall, and some are short. Some are round, and some are thin, and almost everyone at some time or other wants to be something they are not! But as one adviser to teenage girls said, 'You can't live your life worrying that the world is staring at you. When you let people's opinions make you self-conscious you give away your power. . . . The key to feeling [confident] is to always listen to your inner self—[the *real* you.] . . .' Every young woman is a child of destiny and every adult woman a powerful force for good." (*Modesty, Makeovers, and the Pursuit of Physical Beauty*, 17–18). In taking his words to heart, I can testify that his words are just as applicable to all women.

When we are self-conscious about our appearance, it is sometimes simply our perception that is out of order. One woman wrote to me about the way she perceived her family members thought of her. Her negative perception kept her from pursuing opportunities to be with them. Then she experienced a turning point:

"I had finally had it with feeling horrid about myself. I knew I was meant for a better life than I was living. Some kind of divine intervention happened. . . . I was on a flight [after having] just visited my cousin and family for her wedding. I was so nervous to go, because no one had seen me for years [and I dreaded] them see[ing] how big I truly was. However, to my surprise all of my family treated me with love and it turns out I was the one missing out on seeing them. . . . I was overweight, and they loved me anyway. All of a sudden, on that plane ride, I was overcome with emotion, realizing that I was my own worst enemy. I [would] constantly berate myself when I overate and the cycle [would] just keep going. I would give in to my cravings and feel excitement while eating, but right after I finished, I would feel worthless."

Kristen's turning point came when she realized that her self-destructive behaviors came as she allowed others' opinions to shape her perception of herself and make her self-conscious.

What happened after the turning point that came during that flight home especially interested me.

She told me that her life changed in ways that she never would have imagined. She lost 50 pounds in the next year and a half; she took up running and still enjoys it! Her mind is more at ease, and she has learned to coexist with food in a healthy way. The struggle, as it is for many of us, will continue; but being able to feel that love from her family was an incentive and a pivotal point for her.

> *She told me that her life changed in ways that she never would have imagined. She lost 50 pounds in the next year and a half; she took up running and still enjoys it! Her mind is more at ease, and she has learned to coexist with food in a healthy way. The struggle, as it is for many of us, will continue; but being able to feel that love from her family was an incentive and a pivotal point for her.*

I enjoyed hearing about this example of change, which came about not as a result of negative comments from others as well as herself, but from positive, unconditional love, as well as tremendous perseverance. And she took it one step at a time.

Daily we are faced with decisions, and we make them based on a number of influences, among them, what we have learned from others in our past experiences and what we feel, through the Spirit, that we are being directed to do. When we truly learn these lessons, we are better prepared the next time.

Speaking of preparation, Elder Robert D. Hales tells of the time when he was training to be a jet fighter pilot, practicing making crucial decisions in a flight simulator. "I practiced deciding when to bail out of an airplane if the fire warning light came on and I began to spin out of control. I remember one dear friend who didn't make these preparations. He would find a way out of simulator training and then go to play golf or swim. He never learned his emergency procedures! A few months later, fire erupted in his plane, and it spun toward the ground in flames. Noting the fire warning light, his younger companion, having developed a preconditioned response, knew when to bail out of the plane and parachuted to safety. But my friend who had not prepared to make that decision stayed with the plane and died in the crash" ("To the Aaronic Priesthood: Preparing for the Decade of Decision," *Ensign*, May 2007, 48).

Certainly, preparation would have helped the pilot survive. There are many times in our own lives when our preparation is a determining factor in what we are able to achieve. For instance, how well do we think ahead to what we are going to eat during the day? How well do we plan a healthy menu for ourselves and our family? How often do we ask ourselves, "When (not if) am I going to get some physical activity into my day?" We counsel our youth to make decisions before they are actually faced with the situation. How often do we do the same? Do you say to yourself, "I know I'll be at the grocery store today—what am I going to do as I pass by the treats section? Can I not even go down there?" And then there is making a positive decision when faced with a challenge where reaching for extra food, or some other destructive behavior, can be made and help us not to regress.

Although such decisions may seem trivial, they can add up and be lifesaving to many. Anticipating challenges or temptations, we can prepare to meet them, instead of waiting for the crisis to decide how we will react. There will always be stones, boulders, and at times brick walls to face on our road to well-being. If we are blindsided by some circumstance we haven't

> *Anticipating challenges or temptations, we can prepare to meet them, instead of waiting for the crisis to decide how we will react. There will always be stones, boulders, and at times brick walls to face on our road to well-being. If we are blindsided by some circumstance we haven't foreseen and get knocked down, our challenge is to pick ourselves up, dust ourselves off, and keep going.*

foreseen and get knocked down, our challenge is to pick ourselves up, dust ourselves off, and keep going. As we persevere and achieve small victories, we can feel empowered and gain the strength to continue to make positive decisions.

In a general conference address, Elder Joseph B. Wirthlin cited the example of Winston Churchill, who is remembered for his determination as the inspiring leader of Great Britain during World War II: "On one occasion in his later years, he returned to a school where he had studied as a boy. Before he arrived, the headmaster told the students, 'The greatest Britisher of our time is going to come to this school, and I want . . . every one of you to be here with your notebooks. I want you to [write] down what he says, because his speech will be something for you to remember all your lives.' The elderly statesman came in and was introduced. His glasses were down on the end of his nose, as usual. He stood and delivered the following words from an immortal speech that he once gave in Parliament. He said, 'Never, never, never give up.' Then he sat down. That was the speech. It was unmatched. His message was indeed something to be remembered by every boy who heard it and by each of us.

86

We must never give up, regardless of temptations, frustrations, disappointments, or discouragements" ("Never Give Up," *Ensign,* Nov. 1987, 9).

Our greatest example of perseverance is the Savior. He overcame every obstacle in doing the will of our Father in Heaven. Remembering and following His example can help us as we struggle to persevere in the challenges we face, whether physical or spiritual.

We are bombarded, at times, with temptation, although certainly not to the same degree as the Lord. Just as the adversary tempted Him in the wilderness to change stones into bread, kneel down and worship Satan, and demonstrate His divine powers, we too are tempted with food, power, and possessions. At times we get discouraged, but we hang on and make good decisions anyway. There are times in our lives when perseverance means to simply keep moving. We aren't even thinking about gaining any sort of strength from trials in which we may presently find ourselves; and most often we don't realize our increased inner strength until later down the road, after we have had a chance for reflection.

Here is something useful to think about. As you struggle to endure and overcome your challenges, imagine the joy that must have resulted from Christ having persevered. Imagine His dealing with the agony of the cross—how he endured all that

> *Our greatest example of perseverance is the Savior. He overcame every obstacle in doing the will of our Father in Heaven. Remembering and following His example can help us as we struggle to persevere in the challenges we face, whether physical or spiritual.*

He was called to bear, until He was finally able to declare, "It is finished" (John 19:30). Then imagine your own joy in accomplishing the difficult things you are working to achieve. I know that by keeping the Savior's example in our minds and in our hearts, we can persevere and keep moving in the right direction.

As you struggle to endure and overcome your challenges, imagine the joy that must have resulted from Christ having persevered. Then imagine your own joy in accomplishing the difficult things you are working to achieve.

The Jewish holocaust proved to be an unimaginable trial. There are many lessons to be learned from the courageous people who endured those unspeakable atrocities. I find it impossible to understand what millions of men, women, and children must have felt as they were forced to march toward their deaths. In his book *Night*, Elie Wiesel describes the horror of living in various concentration camps during World War II, including Auschwitz and Buchenwald.

He and other prisoners were forced to march from one camp to the next— or as he described it, "running. Like automatons. The SS were running as well, weapons in hand. We looked as though we were running from them." Guards shot those who quit running. Mr. Wiesel describes it this way:

"I was putting one foot in front of the other, like a machine. I was dragging this emaciated body that was still such a weight. If only I could have shed it! Though I tried to put it out of my mind, I couldn't help thinking that there were two of us: my body and I. And I hated that body. I kept repeating to myself: 'Don't think, don't stop, run!'"

Most of us, thankfully, have not been called upon to endure the mental despair and physical agonies caused by war. However, it still goes on. Who cannot be affected by the images of men, women, and their families who are exposed to the atrocities of war as they are reported daily from around the world?

While running or exercising, I have often reached a point where my body has cried out to simply stop and give up. Though such moments only slightly resemble the one described by Mr. Wiesel, when they have occurred, I have often thought about him and told myself, "Don't think, don't stop, run!" In fighting such wars within ourselves, to overcome the mountains in our own mortal missions, we simply need to keep going. Even at times when perhaps we'd rather shed this mortal body.

My daughter Sarah plays high school volleyball. Seeing her so physically active is a miracle to me. She grew up with juvenile rheumatoid arthritis, and there were days where she could barely walk, she was in so much pain. The disease also affected her eyes, and without intervention she could have gone blind. I marvel at the heavenly inspiration that has resulted in modern-day medical treatments, which have enabled Sarah to run, to see, and move her joints as well as she can today.

During one of her recent games, her team was behind. *Way*

> *While running or exercising, I have often reached a point where my body has cried out to simply stop and give up. Though such moments only slightly resemble the one described by Mr. Wiesel, when they have occurred, I have often thought about him and told myself, "Don't think, don't stop, run!"*

behind. Defeat was written all over the faces of the players. The opposing team appeared as if they knew this would be a simple and quick victory. Our girls had lost heart. They had lost their drive. But they kept moving. They worked hard. Then they scored a few points. They began to try a little harder. They won a few more points. However, they still had a long way to go, and time was running out. They reached for the strength that they had momentarily forgotten they had. And that helped to strengthen their teammates. They came back from a seemingly crushing defeat to win the game! The crowd and the team went wild.

After the game, Sarah and I talked about how a combination of a good defense and an effective offense is what ultimately wins the game. Often we find ourselves playing unenthusiastic defense and weak offense in our physical battles. For example, are we incorporating physical activity into our lives? Are we allowing ourselves to eat a few more vegetables? Maybe a little less chocolate? (ouch). Are we doing what we can to ensure our good health? At least trying to get enough sleep? Defense means defending ourselves against the opposition. We can't afford a lack of enthusiasm!

We also can't win any games playing a pathetic offense. Have we decided the time has arrived for us to do something about our physical health? Well, then, let's score some baskets! Let's get that ball to the end zone! We'll get tackled along the way, but we'll be given a lot of chances to keep it going. And, just like that Fiesta Bowl, the game isn't over until the time runs out. Our earthly opportunities aren't over until our scoreboard says it is.

Consider these words by President Gordon B. Hinckley:

"You did not come into this world to fail. You came into the world to succeed. You have accomplished much so far. It is only the beginning. As you move forward on the trail of life, keep the banner of faith in self ever before you. You may not be a genius. You may not be exceptionally smart. But you can be good, and you can try. And you will be amazed at what might happen when in faith you take a step forward" (*One Bright Shining Hope,* [Salt Lake City: Deseret Book, 2006, 152).

I was thinking about our ability to succeed one morning while riding a stationary bicycle. I was watching coverage of the Tour de France, the world's best-known cycling race. Even through the drug scandals that have seemed to plague the sport in the past few years, I still enjoy following the competition. It is a three-week-long road race covering most areas of France and occasionally portions of neighboring countries. Each day during the three weeks, there is a daily winner of each stage of the race.

I was working pretty hard cycling through my imagined passage-ways through Europe as I pictured myself riding right along beside them. But when I looked at these guys on TV, nearing the end of the day's event, I saw passion and perseverance in its finest form. I thought some of those bikes, swaying so hard from side to side, would absolutely fall over from their riders' extreme efforts. The competitors pedaled with incredible speed, strength, and especially determination. It was amazing to watch. They were not there to fail. They were there to succeed. What an inspiration.

Laurel is a friend who has that same determination. She isn't a world-class cyclist; she's a "treadmiller." Yet, as she puts forth the needed effort and carves out time during her busy day to exercise, she shows that same determination to persevere and succeed. She has even lost over 40 pounds during the last year and continues to inspire those around her.

Speaking of inspirational examples, I recently read a sweet story about Elder Neal A. Maxwell and his wife, Colleen. When Elder Maxwell learned in 1996 that he had leukemia, the diagnosis was discouraging, and he seemed willing to submit to his fate. "This attitude explains what looked like pessimism to some in his closest circle. He had worked so long on making himself 'willing to submit' to the Lord (Mosiah 3:19), a verse he had quoted often, that some people thought he was actually too resigned, too ready to yield. . . . Colleen saw things differently, and she didn't hesitate to coach him with the loving directness she had long cultivated. She could see that in his desire to accept what had been allotted to him, he was reluctant to importune the Lord with much pleading. But she pointed out that Jesus' first cry in the Garden of Gethsemane was, 'If it be possible, let this cup pass from me.' . . . With Jesus as our example in all things, she said, it must be permissible to plead. Then of course we submit, as He did. Neal saw her insight and agreed" (Bruce C. Hafen, *A Disciple's Life* [Salt Lake City: Deseret Book Company, 2002], 14–15).

As a result, they pleaded together that his life might be spared. Motivated by their determination, Elder Maxwell's doctor found a new medical treatment that prolonged his life for several years.

Just as a great quarterback, Sister Maxwell was not discouraged by an interception or two. Her faith was sufficient that she

> *Just as a great quarterback, Sister Maxwell was not discouraged by an interception or two. Her faith was sufficient that she refused to give up, and the additional time Elder Maxwell was allotted was a blessing to his family and to the Church.*

refused to give up, and the additional time Elder Maxwell was allotted was a blessing to his family and to the Church. I take great comfort and find determination in the example of his loyal and eternal companion, Colleen.

There is one more story about football and perseverance that I'd like to share. It's Elder Joseph B. Wirthlin's humorous yet profound account of something that happened when he was in high school:

> I'll never forget one high school football game against a rival school. I played the wingback position, and my assignment was to either block the linebacker or try to get open so the quarterback could throw me the ball. The reason I remember this particular game so well is because the fellow on the other side of the line—the man I was supposed to block—was a giant.
>
> I wasn't exactly the tallest athlete in the world. But I think this other guy may have been. I remember looking up at him, thinking he probably weighed as much as two of me. Keep in mind, when I played we didn't have the protective gear that players have today. My helmet was made of leather, and it didn't have a face guard.
>
> The more I thought about it, the more I came to a sobering realization: if I ever let him catch me, I could be cheering for my team the rest of the season from a hospital bed.
>
> Lucky for me, I was fast. And for the better part of the first half, I managed to avoid him.
>
> Except for one play.
>
> Our quarterback dropped back to pass. I was open. He threw the ball, and it sailed towards me.

The only problem was that I could hear a lumbering gallop behind me. In a moment of clarity, I thought that if I caught the ball there was a distinct possibility I could be eating my meals through a tube. But the ball was heading for me, and my team was depending on me. So I reached out, and—at the last instant—I looked up.

And there he was.

I remember the ball hitting my hands. I remember struggling to hang on to it. I remember the sound of the ball falling to the turf. After that, I'm not exactly sure what happened, because the giant hit me so hard I wasn't sure what planet I was on. One thing I did remember was a deep voice coming from behind a dark haze: "Serves you right for being on the wrong team."

William McKinley Oswald was my high school football coach. He was a great coach and had a profound influence on my life. But I think he could have learned his method of motivating players from an army drill sergeant.

That day, during his half-time speech, Coach Oswald reminded the whole team about the pass I had dropped. Then he pointed right at me and said, "How could you do that?"

He wasn't speaking with his inside voice.

"I want to know what made you drop that pass."

I stammered for a moment and then finally decided to tell the truth. "I took my eye off the ball," I said.

The coach looked at me and said, "That's right;

you took your eye off the ball. Don't ever do that again. That kind of mistake loses ball games."

I respected Coach Oswald, and in spite of how terrible I felt, I made up my mind to do what Coach said. I vowed to never take my eye off the ball again, even if it meant getting pounded to Mongolia by the giant on the other side of the line.

We headed back onto the field and started the second half. It was a close game, and even though my team had played well, we were behind by four points late in the fourth quarter.

The quarterback called my number on the next play. I went out again, and again I was open. The ball headed towards me. But this time, the giant was in front of me and in perfect position to intercept the pass.

He reached up, but the ball sailed through his hands. I jumped high, never taking my eye off the ball; stabbed at it; and pulled it down for the game-winning touchdown.

I don't remember much about the celebration after, but I do remember the look on Coach Oswald's face.

"Way to keep your eye on the ball," he said.

(*Press On* [Salt Lake City: Deseret Book Company, 2007], 258–60)

There have been times in my life where, as much as I hate to admit, I've taken my eye off the ball. It's easy to do! But in doing so, I have felt tackled and knocked to the ground, and I've felt my level of perseverance go down with me. It has sometimes taken all my strength to get back up.

Often, however, the thing that impedes our progress isn't a giant linebacker out to get us, such as the one Elder Wirthlin talks about. Sometimes it's a major life occurrence. Often it's simply everyday life. I've felt tackled as I've attempted to complete a project or tried to work through a foot injury that has kept me sidelined. Once in a while it has been a church calling that has seemed overwhelming. Sometimes the laundry tackles me before I know what hit me.

There have been times in my life where, as much as I hate to admit, I've taken my eye off the ball. It's easy to do! But in doing so, I have felt tackled and knocked to the ground, and I've felt my level of perseverance go down with me. It has sometimes taken all my strength to get back up.

These are often not big, scary things (except the laundry). They are the "everyday linebackers" who make it difficult to keep our eyes on the ball. I also wonder if sometimes we aren't trying to keep our eyes on too many balls at once. Which ball matters most? Which ball should we hang onto the hardest? Are there some balls we need to let go so that we can go after the ball that will be eternally worth our effort?

Henry David Thoreau said, "If one advances confidently in the direction of his dreams, and endeavors to live the life which he has imagined, he will meet with a success unexpected in common hours" (*Walden, or Life in the Woods* [New York: Knopf, 1992], 286).

A beautiful testimony of gaining inner strength through perseverance came with Elder Wirthlin's own example during the October 2007 general conference. I happened to attend the Saturday afternoon session when he spoke. I'll have to go back and read his talk again, because the message I received that day came in watching him. Not long into his talk, he began to tremble and strain to speak. Those of us in the audience looked around at one another and then back at him, with concern in our eyes and alarm in our loudly beating hearts. A few days later, his family reported that he had simply locked his knees while standing at the pulpit, and the restricted flow of blood had caused him to lose his strength. However, I was not alone in feeling a little anxious while he spoke. Soon Elder Russell M. Nelson stood up and gently steadied him. As he continued to speak, I was saying to myself, *It's okay, Elder Wirthlin! You can sit down! We understand! You don't have to finish!*

But finish he did. He was not about to quit until he had delivered the message he had prepared. My heart softened as I realized he wasn't going to give up until he had crossed the goal line. Like all good football players, he had help. But he was not about to give up. He wasn't taking his eye off the ball for a second.

> *Inner strength comes when we are willing to persevere. We can pray for increased strength that will come as we demonstrate our willingness to work hard to improve our physical and spiritual health. And it will come. Of that we can be sure!*

Inner strength comes when we are willing to persevere. We can pray for increased strength that will come as we demonstrate our willingness to work hard to improve our physical and spiritual health. And it will come. Of that we can be sure!

Search and Rescue Tips

• Perseverance, in the right direction, builds inner strength. And inner strength can lead to more confidence about our physical bodies, our capacity to serve, and our abilities to learn, as well as promote a more positive self-image.

- Ask: do I let others' opinions of me make me self-conscious to the point of choosing self-destructive behaviors?
- Does your offense or defense need a little coaching? Don't take your eye off the ball!
- As you are trying to make a change to improve your health, strengthen your resolve by reminding yourself, over and over: "I *really* want to accomplish this." "I am willing to do whatever it takes." "I will not let discouragement get me down."
- Learn from your mistakes, pick yourself up, dust yourself off, and keep going. And, never, never, never give up.

CHAPTER SEVEN

Finding Peace While Losing Pride

My brother performed as a knight in his high school's production of *Camelot*. I grew to love the music we seemed to listen to constantly while he was in rehearsals.

In one of the songs, Sir Lancelot presents himself as a perfect knight for King Arthur's Roundtable. Totally lacking in humility, Lancelot unabashedly sings his own praises. After chanting his rhetorical question of where in the world is there a man so "extraordinaire," he replies: "C'est moi! C'est moi."

Lancelot is quite obviously an extreme example of one consumed by pride. He certainly was not deficient in self-appreciation.

Pride is defined this way in *Preach My Gospel:* "To be prideful means to put greater trust in oneself than in God or in His servants. It also means to put the things of the world above the things of God. . . . Pride is competitive; those who are prideful seek to have more and presume they are better than other people. Pride usually results in feelings of anger and hatred, and it is a great stumbling block" (A Guide to Missionary Service [Salt Lake City: The Church of Jesus Christ of Latter-day Saints, 2004], 121).

For years, I erroneously thought that Lancelot personified the only real meaning of pride. Could I be guilty of this sin? Hmmmm. It seemed like everyone else was more perfect than I, particularly in the way they looked, and I assumed, the way they felt about themselves. It was a cold-water, wake-up call when I finally grew up and realized that very few of us feel as if we project a perfect body image. I also realized an important lesson. Pride just isn't thinking that we are better than others. It can also mean feeling that everyone else is better than we are. When we compare ourselves to others, thinking we will never measure up, this, too, is pride. When pride manifests itself in this way, it can also be a real stumbling block and is one of Satan's greatest tools. If he can persuade us to think that we are better than others, it can lead to feelings of arrogance; and if we feel we are not as good as others, it can lead to thoughts of worthlessness. Either way, we offend God, who "resisteth the proud" (James 4:6) and has also declared: "Remember the worth of souls is great in the sight of God" (D&C 18:10).

> Pride just isn't thinking that we are better than others. It can also mean feeling that everyone else is better than we are. When we compare ourselves to others, thinking we will never measure up, this, too, is pride.

I'd like to address this second way of thinking—when we feel we are not as good as others. We are inundated with magazine covers when we simply pass through the grocery store checkout stand. There are more than plenty of photos of famous and not-so-famous people, and articles detailing what they weigh, how they dress, and how they live their lives. I've craned my neck a time or two . . . or three . . . to check them out. I try to do it while I'm lifting groceries out of my cart and onto the moving belt, so it doesn't appear that I'm standing there, staring at them.

However, we don't need a glossy, airbrushed magazine cover to make us feel as though we don't measure up. When we painfully compare ourselves to friends, neighbors, family members, and even Church leaders, we sometimes feel they are far superior to us and that it is futile to think we could ever be perfect or even *acceptable* to our Father in Heaven.

It is true that we have been instructed to "be ye therefore perfect, even as your Father which is in Heaven is perfect" (Matthew 5:48); but gaining perfection is a process, not something to be reached in the next week or month or year. And when we compare ourselves unfavorably to the perceived perfections of others, and become discouraged in doing so, Satan couldn't be happier.

The voices of the world parrot Satan's lies—you are not pretty enough, not thin enough, not wealthy enough—just plain not *good* enough. Satan knows that if he can take something beautiful, like a perfectly toned human body, and hold that up as the ideal, he can make us miserable in our desire to have an "ideal" that was never intended as part of Heavenly Father's plan. Remember, Satan's plan was to make us all the same and "perfect." Heavenly Father understood that Satan's plan of sameness could never lead to happiness or exaltation and rejected it. So should we.

What many of us fail to truly understand is that our physical bodies differ from one another by divine design. Wouldn't this be a boring world if we all looked just alike, wore the same size, had the same hair texture, and even the same color of skin?

What would the effect be if we worked to *appreciate* our differences, rather than define ourselves by them? Becoming too preoccupied with how we present ourselves to the world, we can often experience an overwhelming fear of rejection. That fear can prevent us from being able to focus on what is really important, including our service to and love for others.

> Satan knows that if he can take something beautiful, like a perfectly toned human body, and hold that up as the ideal, he can make us miserable in our desire to have an "ideal" that was never intended as part of Heavenly Father's plan.

I still remember Sister Susan W. Tanner's talk in general conference in the fall of 2005. "Over and over" her mother said to her, "'You must do everything you can to make your appearance pleasing, but the minute you walk out the door, forget yourself and start concentrating on others'" (*Modesty, Makeovers, and the Pursuit of Physical Beauty*, 46). I have begun saying this often, not only to my own daughters before they leave the house, but to myself as well.

Do we heed the voices of our church leaders, rather than those of the world? We need to turn down the world's volume and tune into those voices heading us in the right direction. When King Benjamin addressed his people, he taught about the blessings that can come from heeding the Lord's counsel. The multitude was so numerous and there was so much instruction to offer, he had them pitch their tents around the temple. Each family set up their tent with the door toward the temple, "that thereby they might remain in their tents and hear the words which King Benjamin should speak unto them" (Mosiah 2:6).

Which direction does our tent door face? Is it facing the world, or does it open toward the revealed teachings of heaven? Are we more concerned with how we measure up to the world's standards, or do we put more trust in the Lord? I have found that when we compare ourselves and our abilities to those of others, it is a waste of energy! There is no true peace that can come of that.

I once teamed with three friends to compete in a relay marathon. Each of the four runners was to run just over six miles, completing the 26.2-mile course.

Do we heed the voices of our church leaders, rather than those of the world? We need to turn down the world's volume and tune into those voices heading us in the right direction.

Each leg of the route was a little bit different running experience. I think one of the reasons why it was so enjoyable was because it included friends working together, doing much the same thing, but working in harmony, feeling unity as a team, including a true lack of competitiveness among ourselves.

Jill, our first runner, had the most downhill of the course. While downhill may sound easier, it is often very difficult on the knees. The second person on the relay team is many times the one who doesn't need to be terribly fast, since the rest of the team can make up any time lost on that leg of the race. I was the second runner. Kif came next, and her route ended up being quite confusing and not well marked. She shined. Dianne was last to run, taking it home for us. We all joined up for the last hundred yards and ran across the finish line together. Ruth was going to be part of our team but had to pull out due to a hamstring injury. But she came, sore leg and all, and limped along with us. What a thrill it was to be able to share this wonderful experience together! It sure wasn't as grueling as going it alone, and after having done a few marathons by myself, I could easily see that this was the way a marathon should be run—together, supporting one another, cheering each other, taking over when one member of the team needed to rest, and all of us running as fast and as strongly as we were able. There was a very happy, very peaceful lack of pride in that run. And after each of us did our smaller part, together we celebrated the bigger accomplishment.

I have found that when we compare ourselves and our abilities to those of others, it is a waste of energy! There is no true peace that can come of that.

Wouldn't it be nice if all of the personal marathons in our lives could be run that way? Setting aside our pride and asking for help when we need it? And do we genuinely cheer for each other along the way, without comparing?

Feeling comfortable with ourselves brings a sense of peace. Certainly it takes practice, and that can take time. But it can be done. Think of someone in your own life who seems to be at peace with himself or herself. How does this person react to various situations? What gives him or her that sense of peace? I have a friend who is genuinely happy and cheers for those around her, even though her own life isn't always ideal. She allows herself to be happy for others, without such a concern for how she appears to the world.

Megan is one of the sweet children I came to know and love

as a result of my work in Primary as she was growing up. I was thrilled to hear from her after many years. She has learned many of life's tough lessons. She wrote me a letter about some of her challenges and has given me permission to share her words:

Sometimes you just need to be comfortable in your own skin. That is the lesson that I continue to learn throughout my life as an overweight single adult living in Utah. After returning home from my mission I let myself get caught up in the "why am I not married?" rut. Because of my own insecurities, I threw myself into a life of frenzied mayhem, trying to fill the time that I felt was being wasted by not being a mother, in a culture where motherhood was the highest calling.

I had time-consuming church callings, I was a full-time student, plus I was trying to save the world by being the best part-time nanny, aunt, and president of a community help organization. Having all this to do and doing it all well is the way I defined myself. I seemed to have fooled myself that my worth was contingent upon how busy I was. Unless my life was 24/7 hectic, I seemed to feel *unf*ulfilled and worthless.

> *Feeling comfortable with ourselves brings a sense of peace. Certainly it takes practice, and that can take time. But it can be done.*

By the time I was 25, I had reached my limits. I couldn't do *all* of it anymore. The only way I could see out of the mayhem I had created for myself was to move out on my own. Right away this eliminated some of the stress, but at the same time, it crushed the sense that I had achieved of being "needed."

Just as I felt like I was getting out of this rut, I began to railroad myself again. I accepted a full-time job, even though I was still a full-time student and was tending children on the side. I continued to do it all. I was just as busy as ever and feeling so overwhelmed with it all, I was even stressing out all the people who I was closest to.

That following summer was the loneliest, darkest, hardest time in all my adult life. I was working at a job that I absolutely loved and for which I felt much devotion. I was placed in a position of leadership. But my boss was demeaning and manipulative, and I allowed her to strip every ounce of dignity and self-worth from me. I left that job with nothing left in my tank. I was running on fumes. A week later, I had packed up and moved 1300 miles away to move in with one of my best friends who was attending graduate school. Although it took a few months to convince my mother it was the right decision, I was at peace with my choice.

> *I was living in the middle of nowhere and felt as if I had nothing to contribute. I became an emotional wreck. The strength I had used just months before to hold up the world had all been sucked out of me. I had no ambition, no drive, and sadly, no feeling of self-worth.*

There I was, in an unfamiliar state, with unfamiliar people and nothing, absolutely nothing, to fill my time. I had just made a giant leap into a world that was the complete opposite of how I had been living. Very quickly I allowed Satan to lead me along the same path that my boss had started in the summer, and I got more and more down on myself. I felt so unfulfilled. I was living in the middle of nowhere and felt as if I had nothing to contribute. I became an emotional wreck. The strength I had used just months before to hold up the world had all been sucked out of me. I had no ambition, no drive, and sadly, no feeling of self-worth.

> "What is more important is that we are at peace with the Lord and with what He expects of us—to be comfortable in our own skin and serve in whatever capacity we are able, with the talents we have been given."

I had lost myself. I was glad my best friend was with me, but I had an opportunity to spend some solitary moments reflecting on my life, my loves, and my desires. I decided to work harder on being comfortable with myself. I returned to the basic truths that I have always known—that there is no optimum size or person. We can improve ourselves by setting aside our pride, being patient with ourselves, and feeling peace, one step at a time. By small means are great things brought to pass.

I didn't want to let people like the boss I'd had affect me in such a negative way anymore. I resolved that I would not give people the power to hurt me. I wanted to go home and be with the people I love. I wanted to face my fears of not being good enough. Of course they all welcomed me with open arms, and the fear that I had created left me immediately. It is not so important the number of people we have served during the week or how many hours we have logged at a local charity, or even what others think of us. What is more important is that we are at peace with the Lord and with what He expects of us—To be comfortable in our own skin and serve in whatever capacity we are able, with the talents we have been given.

Feeling at peace also requires that we feel the Savior's love in the midst of all these earthly trials. We can make it, knowing the Savior is there, along the way, with His arms out-stretched.

With the help of my Father in Heaven, I found the courage to let the resentment go. I also released the feeling of not feeling accepted in this "body-image world." It helped me in my eternal quest to conquer those inner demons that try to make me less than what my Heavenly Father has created. Parts of me were healed that I didn't even know needed healing.

Megan's quest took courage, patience, and even putting aside feelings of pride that can affect us all. I admire her and am thrilled she feels more at peace.

Megan mentioned many of the elements of feeling at peace with ourselves. Those qualities include being at peace with the Lord and what He expects of us. She also talked about being patient with ourselves and our efforts and not giving others the power to hurt us. She was able to reflect on her blessings and the positive things happening in her life. I have also found that gratitude and hope can bring such peace.

Feeling at peace also requires that we feel the Savior's love in the midst of all these earthly trials. We can make it, knowing the Savior is there, along the way, with His arms outstretched. Sister Kathleen H. Hughes has given us this comforting reassurance: "I recognize how true it is that life often feels like a great pile of obligations, frustrations, and disappointments. But the Lord is there, always the same, His arms still outstretched. When we feel overwhelmed, we have to *remember* the peace He has spoken to us on previous occasions. *His* peace brings comfort and strength; the world cannot give that to us" ("Remembering the Lord's Love," *Ensign*, Nov. 2006, 111–12; emphasis in original).

> *There is no greater example of the way in which we should perceive ourselves and our mission here on earth than that of the Savior. And, doing the Lord's will brings greater happiness than can ever be found in the fleeting pleasures of the world.*

The idea that the Lord does not love us if we are not perfect is one of Satan's insidious ploys. So is the notion that we are here to achieve success and happiness on our own, without the Lord's help. Nothing could be further from the truth. The Savior wants us to succeed. As Truman G. Madsen so eloquently put it, "His Spirit, like the Savior himself, is not sent into the world to condemn the world, but to lift us. He is not interested in putting us down. The gifts and the fruits of the Spirit engulf all our deepest needs, whatever our present desires: insight, flashes of guidance, energy, all the virtues that center in Christ, and through them, all the fire that purifies our feelings and our aspirations. . . . Why do we think we can do it alone? And why do we turn our back on him when we need him most? . . . The Savior has power to change us even when circumstances remain the same" ("The Savior, the Sacrament, and Self-Worth," 247–48).

There is no greater example of the way in which we should perceive ourselves and our mission here on earth than that of the Savior. And, doing the Lord's will brings greater happiness than can ever be found in the fleeting pleasures of the world.

We can have peaceful reassurance, knowing that we have done everything in our power—not to bring back the best body according to the world's standards, but to bring back that which He gave us, after caring for it, protecting it, and striving to live up to the standards He has set.

Finally, during the Savior's ministry, He did not attempt to find acceptance or to gain love from others by conforming to what He knew people would approve. Some chose to follow Him, others chose a different path. He came into the world to do the will of the Father (see 3 Nephi 27:13). But His actions were not dependent on what others thought of Him We can emulate the Savior's example by not making our actions dependent on what others think of us.

Jesus declared: "Peace I leave with you, my peace I give unto you: not as the world giveth, give I unto you. Let not your heart be troubled, neither let it be afraid" (John 14:27). I'm convinced that He wants us to feel peaceful about ourselves. Finding such peace takes diligence, hard work, and especially patience, and at times it may seem as if it is a never-ending process. We may never sit at a knight's—or anyone else's—"roundtable." But we can continue learning, and we can live in the presence of our Father in Heaven someday, bringing this physical body back to Him. We can have peaceful reassurance, knowing that we have done everything in our power—not to bring back the best body according to the world's standards, but to bring back that which He gave us, after caring for it, protecting it, and striving to live up to the standards He has set.

Instead of allowing the pride and reflection of the world's mirror to guide us, we will feel lasting peace when we allow the Spirit to lead us and to become our beacon.

Search and Rescue Tips

Ask:

- What areas in my life are affected by pride? Do I find that I often compare myself with others?
- What can I do to put the things of God above the things of the world?
- Where do I need to refocus so that I can feel greater peace?
- How can feeling better about myself enable me to feel more at peace with myself?

Then:

- Instead of trying to be the best, try seeking to *be your own personal* best.

CHAPTER EIGHT

Finding Our Way to Nineveh

One Sunday afternoon, my daughter Hillary came home from Primary with a puzzle she had received as an activity that day. At the bottom of the sheet was the word *Start,* and at the top was the destination *Nineveh.* The puzzle was a maze, through which the Primary children were to figure out how to get to Nineveh. They had obviously been studying the Old Testament story of Jonah, to whom the Lord had given instructions to go preach to the wicked people of Nineveh. Afraid and reluctant to go to the sinful city, Jonah had instead hopped on a ship bound for Tarshish. En route, the ship was tossed around in a mighty tempest, and Jonah realized that his procrastination and unwillingness to do the Lord's will was putting other men's lives in danger as well. As soon as he was cast overboard, the sea calmed. It was then that Jonah had a three-day stay in the belly of a big fish. I would think that by that time, Jonah was wishing he had just gone to Nineveh in the first place. When the fish finally spewed him out onto dry land, he went on to fulfill his mission.

The Old Testament account indicates that Jonah was surprised when the wicked people there actually heeded his words and repented. There is more to the story, but Jonah did end up finding his way to Nineveh.

Where is our Nineveh? Perhaps it is a place where, when we get there, we will know we have triumphed over an obstacle, great or small. If we are to reach our destination, are there changes we know we need to make—particularly in the way we see and feel about ourselves? Perhaps the goal is achieving a healthy weight. Maybe it's increasing our exercise. Maybe it's changing our lifestyle and eating more nutritiously. It could be simply feeling better about ourselves.

Jonah foolishly hoped he could flee from the presence of the Lord. I think, deep down, though, he knew that he couldn't really escape. He knew what the Lord wanted him to do. He was trying anything he could *not* to do it.

What is preventing us from getting to our Ninevehs? Are we following Jonah's example of procrastination and rationalization? Not wanting to face what lies ahead, even when we know what the blessings of Nineveh will bring? Even when we know we need to make a change, we may be quite willing to make excuses and delay our departure. Certainly, there are instances when our time and energy levels make it inconvenient to act. Disease or illness may also strike. There are competing priorities. Perhaps, as much as we hate to admit it, we simply don't want to change badly enough. Maybe we feel too tired. Are we discouraged? Maybe we need to ask ourselves if it is high enough on our priority list. Could it be time to move it up higher? Perhaps it is simply time to quit making excuses and get going! Like a swimmer who is reluctant to get into the water, we can stand forever on the side of the pool, thinking about all the reasons we don't want to jump in, or we can simply take the plunge.

As silly as it sounds, one of my excuses for not exercising was that I already had so much laundry to do; I did not want to have to wash even one more dirty shirt! I have worked hard to change my thinking over the years, to the point that the "one more dirty shirt" is now my trophy, my reward for a great workout. (I will probably never get a trophy from winning any marathons, so that dirty shirt will have to do.)

Sadly, our teenage son, Stephen, had a similar aversion to doing laundry. He came home, after five months of 7th grade PE, and proudly showed me his gym clothes. "Mom!" he exclaimed, "I went for two whole terms without ever bringing my PE clothes home to wash!" His sisters about passed out. It was one of those proud mothering moments. Of course I wondered how I could go the entire semester without realizing his stinky outfit had never made it home to the washer. While trying to smile at his valiant effort to achieve a perfect, albeit smelly, record, I made a mental note to apologize to his PE teacher. Was he just not doing what he knew he should do, or was he really going for that lovely, lofty goal?

Equally debilitating as making excuses is rationalizing our behavior. We like to explain our actions to the point of staying

> *Equally debilitating as making excuses is rationalizing our behavior. We like to explain our actions to the point of staying right there, in our comfort zone. We may even like placing the blame elsewhere for our failure to act.*

right there, in our comfort zone. We may even like placing the blame elsewhere for our failure to act.

When our daughter Hillary was a young girl, she had an imaginary friend she called "Brittany" who was constantly by her side. No one but Hillary could see Brittany, but there was no end to the stories Hillary told us about her adventures with her friend. Hillary would sit outside on the lawn and "visit" with Brittany. In her purse, she'd tuck her favorite little book, *Stand a Little Taller,* by President Gordon B. Hinckley, and she would take walks around the neighborhood, often pausing to turn to her imaginary friend to emphasize a point. She could get quite animated. Hillary would come to us with tales of Brittany's latest adventures or stories "Brittany had told her." It was all so innocent and endearing.

One incident was especially amusing. Hillary had done something naughty, although now I can't even remember what it might have been. I asked her a question that, from all the parenting books I'd read, I shouldn't have asked her at her age: "Why did you do that?" I inquired. She looked at me and very solemnly responded, "Brittany did it." My anger quickly vanished, and I tried not to let her see me smile.

"Mom, I'm serious. It was Brittany!"

"Go get Brittany," I played along. "I need to have a little chat with her."

Hillary turned to go, and then looked back at me very puzzled. After we had shared a good laugh, I talked to her about telling the truth, about how although it was okay to have an imaginary friend at that time in her life, honesty was also a very important principle. It was a sweet childhood moment.

While avoiding some task we perceive as unpleasant, it's easy, or at least much more comfortable, to place the blame somewhere else. To rationalize our behavior. To say, "Brittany did it."

So we can procrastinate and we can rationalize our behavior, but what else can delay us on our road to Nineveh? It is also easy to get distracted.

One of our children's favorite picture books is *If You Give a Mouse a Cookie*, written by Laura Joffe Numeroff. The story begins when a boy offers a mouse a cookie. The mouse then asks for a glass of milk to go with it. As the boy pours him some milk, the mouse also asks for a straw, then a napkin. When he looks in the mirror to make sure he doesn't have a milk mustache, the mouse notices his hair needs a trim. Throughout the story, the mouse begins one thing and then notices other projects to be done. He keeps the boy busy getting a broom for sweeping, crayons and paper for drawing, a box and blanket for napping. Finally, after changing direction with each page, the mouse gets thirsty and asks for a glass of milk. Then he realizes he wants a cookie to go with it. And so the cycle continues.

> *While avoiding some task we perceive as unpleasant, it's easy, or at least much more comfortable, to place the blame somewhere else. To rationalize our behavior. To say, "Brittany did it."*

Many days I feel like that mouse. I begin one thing and then get distracted by a million other things, most of them good, and each one needs doing.

For instance, one morning, not long ago, I put on my workout clothes and was making my way downstairs to the treadmill. As I thought about the workout my legs were going to "enjoy" that morning, I noticed dishes in the sink. It wouldn't take me very long to just throw those in the dishwasher, would it? Then

I could be at least a little ahead in my day. And why didn't they get done last night? Oh, that reminds me. I was supposed to call Sister Taylor back. No, I won't do it right now. I'm headed downstairs. I'll just write myself a note and do it after working out. Where is some paper? There's very little chance of finding a pen that works, but what about a pencil? Oh, this one needs to be sharpened. Why won't this sharpener work? Look how full the little container thing is.

Going over to empty it, I notice how full the kitchen garbage can is. Something stinky is in it, too. Ewwww. I'll just quickly run out and empty it. The phone rings, and I let it go. Then on my way out to the garbage can, I see my neighbor outside. She hasn't been feeling well, and I haven't seen her for weeks. This is a perfect opportunity to go see how she's doing. As I walk over to see her, I can't help noticing some weeds that are getting way too long. I pull them as we talk. My short chat with my neighbor turns into a realization that I haven't finished some Relief Society issues and that a few sisters are waiting on me. I'll have to add that to the list, if I can find the paper and get this pencil sharpened. I decide I'll sweep up those weeds later. I wave good-bye to my neighbor, go back into the house, hear the phone ringing, and decide to ignore it again.

On my way through the utility room, I trip over the piles of laundry by the washing machine and notice that the loads are now ready for switching. Since the piles reach into the kitchen, I stop to quickly switch loads. The phone rings again. Before I pick it up, I notice on the caller ID that it is the school—I'd better answer that. I'm told that Hillary is sick, and can I come pick her up?

Concerned for my daughter, I throw on some long sweats before I traipse over to the elementary school. Poor little thing.

She's got another bad sore throat, and I wonder if I should take her to the doctor again. Or will it work itself out? Did I even comb my hair before coming over here? Maybe I should call the doctor and make an appointment—they fill up so quickly. As I'm calling the doctor, I remember I still haven't called for a desperately needed haircut.

Amy texts me. "What's for dinner?" she asks. And can her friend Brad come over to eat, too? I tell her I haven't even thought that far. Didn't I vow, at one time, to plan out the week's meals ahead of time?

I'm home now with Hillary. She smiles at me as I give her hugs and some sore throat spray. I read her a story and tuck her in as she drifts off to sleep.

There's the buzzer! The clothes are dry. As I quickly pull them out, I see my favorite workout shirt, all clean and fresh. Holding up the shirt, I sigh heavily and think about my thighs, and I realize the treadmill is still waiting for me . . .

My morning might have gone differently if I had at least begun a little earlier. I could have gone straight down to the treadmill, bypassing the sink full of dishes, and grabbed a pen or even a crayon, without stopping to empty the pencil sharpener. I would have been able to exercise and then been available to care for Hillary—both of which are very important to me. It's not that I am seeking such toned thighs (although maybe I should be); but, I feel, regular workouts are essential to my physical as well as my mental health.

But that morning, as well as other mornings, could there have been another reason that I didn't go straight down to exercise? That reason sometimes includes a little "I don't want to" attitude, which leads to seeking for excuses, rationalizing my behavior, however well-intended it may be, and procrastinating.

It's simply hard, many times, to get moving, get sweating, get pushing harder. Certainly the easier route is to find a way out of accomplishing our goal. Jonah decided to try doing what he could to avoid facing the task ahead of him. Nineveh wasn't in his comfort zone, and he didn't want to go there.

So. How do we get to Nineveh? There are different roads that begin from where we are, leading to our destination. Some are direct routes. Others wind up and over; still others are full of more rocks in the road. Every once in a while we need to stop and look around. Are we spending the majority of our time and effort to get there? What can we do to refocus on the road and head to our destination? And on days when we can't get very far, are we "beating ourselves up"? That certainly can be harmful, in that it can lead to giving up completely on trying to make the positive changes we want to make.

> *Jonah decided to try doing what he could to avoid facing the task ahead of him. Nineveh wasn't in his comfort zone, and he didn't want to go there.*

I know my husband and children would rather have a happy wife and mother than a spotlessly clean house. And there will always be something to wash. I once e-mailed my friend and asked, "The laundry—when does it all end?" Her response was, "In the cemetery!" The laundry, at least for now, will always be there. However, endorphins will flow much more freely—we will be much happier women and men, in all our roles—if we can take a little time along the road to get our hearts beating, our lungs working, and to burn a few calories.

Finding our way to Nineveh requires becoming willing to do what we need to do to get there. How badly do we want to get going? Are we willing to stay pointed in the right direction? It takes just one step at a time to get there. Sometimes those steps feel like a marathon.

I have found it encouraging to focus on how I will feel *after* the workout, instead of the difficulty of getting there. Actually picturing in my mind all those fat cells diminishing, the toxins flying out of my body, and the muscles getting firmer as I go helps keep me moving. I've also found that watching a favorite TV show helps to pass the time on the treadmill. It also keeps my mind off any unpleasantness! Certainly planning the time for a workout as part of my day has been an effective tool in getting it done, and making activity part of my day has actually gotten easier to do the more I do.

My friend Rosie often says, "I've never heard anyone, when they've finished exercising, say that they regret the time spent working out."

There will be certain detours. Circumstances will come up where, at least for a while, you may have to set aside some of your "personal enhancement goals." As I have trained for and run three marathons, I realize what a demanding amount of time that takes.

I know my husband and children would rather have a happy wife and mother than a spotlessly clean house. And there will always be something to wash. I once e-mailed my friend and asked, "The laundry— when does it all end?" Her response was, "In the cemetery!"

As much as I enjoy doing that (okay, many times it's not until *after* the training runs are over), it takes an incredible amount of time and effort.

A few years ago I was training for the St. George Marathon, held every fall. I was also trying to juggle the demands of having three teenagers as well as two younger children. That summer before the marathon was full of scheduled training runs. Amy had recently turned sixteen, and she was socializing her little self right up to the latest possible minute of her curfew. Often, when she got home at night, we had some wonderful talks. She was born a night owl, much to my chagrin and that of my sweet farm-boy husband. Both of us would rather follow the "early to bed, early to rise" way of life.

But those late evening hours were when she wanted to share her thoughts and feelings with me. There is so much that goes on in a young woman's life, and I genuinely enjoy hearing all about the dreams and the drama. That summer, many a wonderful chat would happen when she got home, although I would almost have to prop up my eyelids with toothpicks to stay awake. Some nights I wanted to hurry her through our conversation; after all, I had a difficult, twelve-mile run to cover early the next morning! So although I would have preferred to move our talks to an earlier hour, those were the times she opened her heart to me.

I finally realized, about halfway through my sixteen-week training plan, that at that point in my life, I would rather stay up and be there for her than run the marathon. There would always be more marathons. But the times my daughter wants to talk to me are precious to me. I am willing to do all in my power to ensure that open communication. Sometimes it comes at quite a high price. But I didn't want to miss a single moment of those precious talks.

I pulled out of the marathon that year. Although I experienced some yearnings to participate as it got closer, I was happier (and okay, relieved) to have devoted my time that summer to something else I really wanted to do.

So my trip to Nineveh was put on hold that summer. And yet, I was still going where I wanted and needed to go. Flexibility is necessary. But ask yourself, over and over, "What is really important here?" "How badly do I want it?" If you want it that bad, hang in there and work to clear away the distractions until you have achieved that which will get you closer to Nineveh. The distractions will always be there. And they could all be *good* distractions! But what is highest on your priority list? In putting that at the top, how can you spend the time and effort to work so those items get done?

> *Distractions will always be there. And they could all be* good *distractions! But what is highest on your priority list? In putting that at the top, how can you spend the time and effort to work so those items get done?*

Aside from caring for my husband and family, three things at the top of my daily Nineveh List include:

- Scripture reading
- Personal prayer
- Exercise

I have more on my list. But these three, in caring for myself, are at the top. I've found that if I make my list too long, I get overwhelmed. But if I can just get those three things done each day, I am a much more effective, happier, and healthier person.

In spite of what I have said, there are legitimate detours on the road to Nineveh, and it may take a while to get there. We may occasionally longingly gaze at other paths that seem more fun to travel, but we can be content as we find happiness and hope on our own route, rather than wishing it all away or making continual excuses for being on the side of the road. And running alongside us, there will always be a mouse or two wanting us to stop and get them a cookie. Unless they're starving, they can wait. And although it will be tempting to rationalize our behavior by blaming "Brittany" or anything or anybody else, we can find strength and courage to keep moving. Let's get going. Nineveh is waiting!

Search and Rescue Tips

- Ask: What is my "Nineveh"? What do I need to do to get there? Am I willing to do what it takes?
- What excuses am I making? Are any of them honestly valid ones for preventing me from making a needed change? Can I work around them?
- Try this. Fold a regular-sized sheet of paper in half. On the left side, write at the top, "*Priorities.*" Be specific. Include health (physical) priorities, personal and family priorities, spiritual priorities, and social (including professional and financial) priorities. Then, on the right side, write at the top, "*Where I Spend My Time.*" Write down how you spend your time each day. Now compare the two sides. How well do they match up? Priorities will no doubt change as our circumstances change. But right now—do you need to adjust your time and your priorities so that they are more in harmony?

CHAPTER NINE

Finding Faith and Miracles

I can testify that in seeking to improve our physical bodies through proper care, exercise, and nutrition, that faith is truly a principle of action and power. If we believe it to be possible, we can see miracles in our lives, for I have discovered that the road to better health is definitely a spiritual one.

Certainly there will always be loud worldly voices telling us the way we need to look, and I hope we've already established that we are foolish to heed everything they say. But we need to be honest with ourselves. In sincere and healthy introspection of our bodies, are there features we need to improve? There are a small number of women who are truly happy and content with the shape and size of their bodies. Most of us are not. And although having the perfect physical body seems impossible in this life, we can and should do what we can to improve our health and well-being.

Every so often we get a wake-up call that helps us to see we are not where we want to be. That call may even cause us to change course. There are a variety of incentives. As Caroline Schoeder has observed: "Some people change their ways when they see the light; others when they feel the heat" (thinkexist.com). Perhaps this book will help you make that decision.

I realized one evening the importance of changing course, hoping for a miracle, and exercising greater faith. Usually it's not in that particular order, but this time it was. My sister Jill had moved into a townhouse, and I went to see her in an unfamiliar neighborhood. After our visit, she told me how to find my way back to the freeway. But it was a dark, moonless night, and with the disappearing streetlights, I soon lost my way. Finding myself on a bumpy, deserted road, I stopped the car, and with my foot on the brake began looking around to get my bearings.

Suddenly, a huge headlight loomed up at me out of the darkness, and I heard a deafeningly loud horn. I had stopped on some railroad tracks, and I looked out of my car window to see a train coming right at me! Pure adrenaline made me scream and stomp on the accelerator. As the train roared on by, I sat there in the dark, trying to catch my breath. Then, with my heart still pounding, I called my sister, and after I calmed down, we had a good laugh. She also gave me instructions on how to get back on the right road.

The train's loud horn and bright light were the incentive for me to change course (and do so immediately). And I was grateful for the miracle that I wasn't killed. I was also grateful I could exercise my faith by seeking for help and knowing I could get back, even though I didn't have a clue where I was.

Faith and miracles are essential as we seek to change our

direction—toward better health and improved feelings about ourselves. Sometimes we feel hopeless. That change is impossible. We've let things go for so long, or we are too deeply engrained in bad habits, that we think it's too late. We think it's too difficult. That is when we need to put our trust in the Lord, that He can and will help us make those changes. Perhaps there is a miracle in store.

Looking at ourselves and at the changes we need to make need not be total drudgery. For instance, just recently I heard a woman say lightheartedly that the reason she wants to lose weight is so that her grandsons will be able to lift her casket.

And just a few months ago, I met members of a charming group of women in North Carolina who call themselves WISE, which stands for "Women in Shape, Eventually." They meet for support and encouragement. What a delightful name! It shows a promise of hope and expectation.

> *Many of us don't want to attain eventually. We want things right now! We live in an age of immediate gratification. We want magic pills and potions for weight loss, better sleep, for staying alert, more muscle, less fat, and every other obstacle that stands in our way.*

Many of us don't want to attain *eventually*. We want things right now! We live in an age of immediate gratification. We want magic pills and potions for weight loss, better sleep, for staying alert, more muscle, less fat, and for every other obstacle that stands in our way. We want assurance today for a happier tomorrow. But are we willing to exercise the faith and work hard to make the necessary changes?

President Boyd K. Packer relates this helpful story:

Shortly after I was called as a General Authority, I went to Elder Harold B. Lee for counsel. He listened very carefully to my problem and suggested that I see President David O. McKay. President McKay counseled me as to the direction I should go. I was very willing to be obedient but saw no possible way for me to do as he counseled me to do.

I returned to Elder Lee and told him that I saw no way to move in the direction I was counseled to go. He said, "The trouble with you is you want to see the end from the beginning." I replied that I would like to see at least a step or two ahead. Then came the lesson of a lifetime: "You must learn to walk to the edge of the light, and then a few steps into the darkness, then the light will appear and show the way before you."

(*Memorable Stories with a Message* [Salt Lake City: Deseret Book Company, 2000], 33)

> As we take care of our physical bodies, we can pray for much needed strength. Then, as Joseph did with the plates, we can also seek to keep our bodies out of situations where there is "malicious intent."

To move ahead when we can't see takes faith. The LDS Bible Dictionary describes faith as "a principle of action and of power, . . . true faith always moves its possessor to some kind of physical and mental action; it carries an assurance of the fulfillment of the things hoped for" (670).

We demonstrate our faith as we take action. A good example is found in Joseph Smith, who did not simply pray that the gold plates would be protected in his care; he actively took every precaution to assure that they did not fall into the hands of those with malicious intent. He creatively came up with ways, under the direction of Heavenly Father, to guarantee the plates would serve their purpose while under his watch.

As we take care of our physical bodies, we can pray for much needed strength. Then, as Joseph did with the plates, we can also seek to keep our bodies out of situations where there is "malicious intent." Too much chocolate cake? Perhaps. But in all seriousness, recognizing and avoiding situations and substances that will harm our bodies or get in the way of our goal is of utmost importance.

Elder Russell M. Nelson said, "Remarkable as your body is, its prime purpose is of even greater importance—to serve as tenement for your spirit. . . . Not an age in life passes without temptation, trial, or torment experienced through your physical body. But as you prayerfully develop self-mastery, desires of the flesh may be subdued. And when that has been achieved, you may have the strength to submit to your Heavenly Father, as did Jesus, who said, 'Not my will, but thine, be done'" (Luke 22:42). (As quoted in Melanie Douglass, *Losing It!* [Salt Lake City: Deseret Book Company, 2005], 16–17.)

We get better at this as we gain experience. And often, it just takes a little maturity as we continue to exercise faith to notice that even small miracles have occurred in our lives.

We get better at this as we gain experience. And often, it just takes a little maturity as we continue to exercise faith to notice that even small miracles have occurred in our lives. Miracles of how we regard our physical bodies.

Miracles of how we regard our physical bodies. Take Elder M. Russell Ballard's reference to "A Woman's Lifeline":

Age 3: She looks at herself and sees a queen.

Age 8: She looks at herself and sees Cinderella.

Age 15: She looks at herself and sees an ugly duckling (Mom, I can't go to school looking like this today!).

Age 20: She looks at herself and sees "too fat/too thin, too short/too tall, too straight/too curly" but decides she's going out anyway.

Age 30: She looks at herself and sees "too fat/too thin, too short/too tall, too straight/too curly" but decides she doesn't have time to fix it so she's going out anyway.

Age 40: She looks at herself and sees "too fat/too thin, too short/too tall, too straight/too curly" but says, "At least I am clean," and goes out anyway.

Age 50: She looks at herself and says, "I am what I am," and goes wherever she wants to go.

Age 60: She looks at herself and reminds herself of all the people who can't even see themselves in the mirror anymore. Goes out and conquers the world.

Age 70: She looks at herself and sees wisdom, laughter, and ability and goes out and enjoys life.

Age 80: Doesn't bother to look. Just puts on a purple hat and goes out to have fun with the world.

The moral is, maybe we should all grab that purple hat a little earlier.

(*Ye Shall Bear Record of Me*, "Here Am I, Send Me" [Salt Lake City: Bookcraft, 2002], 316–17)

I smile now when I see women wearing purple hats. I've got to get one!

But there is an important message there. We are able to see ourselves differently as we submit to the will of our Father in Heaven. Interestingly, I have found that submission comes more easily the more I develop self-mastery. One way to develop self-mastery is by strengthening our core—our spiritual, physical, and our emotional foundation. A favorite Primary song, "The Wise Man and the Foolish Man," is based on a passage in Matthew, chapter 7.

> *The wise man built his house upon the rock,*
> *And the rains came tumbling down. . . .*
> *The rains came down, and the floods came up,*
> *And the house on the rock stood still. . . .*
> *The foolish man built his house upon the sand,*
> *And the rains came tumbling down. . . .*
> *The rains came down, and the floods came up,*
> *And the house on the sand washed away.*
> (*Children's Songbook*, p. 281)

Jesus had been teaching the Sermon on the Mount. In verse 24, He states, "Therefore whosoever heareth these sayings of mine, and doeth them, I will liken him unto a wise man, which built his house upon a rock . . ."

In the Bible version the Savior explains the difference between the wise man and the foolish man. Both men built a house. Nothing is mentioned about the beauty or size of each. The difference was in the foundation.

When "the rain descended, and the floods came, and the winds blew, and beat upon that house"; the house did not fall, "for it was founded upon a rock" (v. 25).

The foolish man's house was subjected to the same earthly elements. But because he had built his house upon the sand, not only did his house fall, but "great was the fall of it" (v. 27).

Jesus likened the foolish man to "every one that heareth these sayings of mine, and doeth them not" (v. 26).

The lesson is plain: the strength of a home lies not in its size or beauty but in the sureness of its foundation. Likewise, the strength of our testimony depends on the foundation of faith that we have laid.

> The lesson is plain: the strength of a home lies not in its size or beauty but in the sureness of its foundation. Likewise, the strength of our testimony depends on the foundation of faith that we have laid.

All of us have experienced or will experience challenges with our physical bodies. Communicable diseases, genetic inheritance, the environment, and habits all have an effect. These physical challenges can affect us mentally as well. They can also influence our spiritual development. But as we work hard on improvement, we need to pay particular attention to securing our foundations.

I love the parable C. S. Lewis tells: "Imagine yourself as a living house. God comes in to rebuild that house. At first, perhaps, you can understand what He is doing. He is getting the drains right and stopping the leaks in the roof and so on: you knew that those jobs needed doing and so you are not surprised. But presently he starts knocking the house about in a way that hurts abominably and does not seem to make sense. What on earth is He up to? The explanation is that He is building quite a different house from the one you thought of—throwing out a new wing here, putting on an extra floor there, running up towers, making courtyards. You thought you were going to be made into a decent little cottage: but He is building a palace" (*Mere Christianity* [New York: HarperSan Francisco, 2001], 205).

I have another sister, Chris, who is in the process of building a home. I've witnessed the countless decisions, preparations, and tasks, both major and minor, which have been made in the process. Chris and her husband have involved their children in much of the building, even before the foundation was laid. Their teenage sons have spent many hours pounding nails, setting up frames, and raising beams. The younger children have helped to move brick, clear debris, and carry simple tools and supplies. They have had to commit to working long hours to achieve their dream. It has been quite a process.

The outward appearance of a home is what gets noticed first. Not particularly the strength of its walls or foundation. But those will be most evident as the home continues to age, protecting that which is within from the fierce, beating elements outside.

Our well-being is much the same. We need to be vigilant caretakers of our good health—physical, emotional, and spiritual. Some days are certainly easier than others, but to use Lewis's analogy, we will be assailed—whether by failing health, accidents, changing circumstances, and if nothing else, advancing years. The strength of our spiritual foundation (which is a function of faith) will determine how well we will stand. And every day we make choices. Choices, for better or worse, which affect our health and our self-image.

As I was running my first marathon, down the same canyon the pioneers used to enter the Salt Lake Valley, I felt a real connection to the Saints, who exhibited faith and diligence as they made preparations, then forged across the plains to Utah. My great-great-great-grandfather, Appleton Milo Harmon, was a member of the first wagon train company. He was a skillful mechanic who along with William Clayton was asked to construct an odometer. William Clayton's journal describes that wooden device as being constructed upon "the principle of the endless screw." Its revolutions enabled the pioneers to accurately measure the distance traveled, which must have been a great aid to those wagon trains that came later (see B. H. Roberts, *A Comprehensive History of the Church*, 3:175).

Like the pioneers, faith drives our willingness to work hard to get us where we want to go. How grateful I am for the records that the pioneers kept. Reading them, we can more fully understand the faith they possessed and the diligence they practiced.

On the banks of the Mississippi River, at the western end of Parley Street, is a historical marker, including a reproduced page from the journal of my ancestor Appleton. Recently our family stood on the banks of that mighty river. Mark and I tried to impress upon our children what it may have felt like to be among the Saints who stood on that very spot before they crossed the river, after being driven out of their homes, seeing their beautiful temple being destroyed, and knowing they had a difficult journey ahead of them, including possible death. Although I'm not sure our children fully appreciated what we were trying to teach, hopefully they will remember the sacred feeling that abounds there.

Like the pioneers, faith drives *our* willingness to work hard to get us where we want to go. How grateful I am for the records the pioneers kept. Reading their words, we can more fully understand the faith they possessed and the diligence they practiced. Faith enabled Appleton and his family to join the other pioneers in making the amazing journey, but he was also able to help others along the way and those who were part of the wagon trains to come.

I love the words of the hymn, "They, the Builders of the Nation":

> They, the builders of the nation,
> Blazing trails along the way;
> Stepping-stones for generations
> Were their deeds of ev'ry day.
> Building new and firm foundations,
> Pushing on the wild frontier,
> Forging onward, ever onward,
> Blessed, honored Pioneer!
> (Hymns, no. 36)

Imagine the faith it took to step out into a land that had been largely unexplored, not knowing either the length of the journey or the final destination. Certainly those early Saints were sustained by the Spirit as they trudged forward through their incredible physical trials. We so admire their examples. But as modern-day pioneers, we also need to have the Spirit as we make choices every day, pushing forward to build our own new and firm foundations in the face of our different but sometimes equally demanding challenges.

Faith makes miracles possible—physical, emotional, and spiritual miracles. Often, the miracle comes only after we have taken those first few steps ahead into the darkness, or after we have been through a hot refiner's fire.

I recently visited with Linda, a sweet neighbor who has been ill for many years. I held her hand and we shared a laugh as I gently teased her about having spent so much time in the hospital that they were going to name one of the wings after her. I marveled that she is still able to find humor in her situation, but wasn't really surprised. Linda knows where she is headed and with her cheerful attitude has learned to take life a day at a time. She also has a wonderfully supportive family. They are people of faith, and even through all that they have experienced, she and her family members still look for the beauty in the storm. They understand the concept that "doubt and fear are opposed to faith" (*Preach My Gospel*, 116).

There are times when, although we pray for what we want, we understand and finally accept the Lord's will. Over the past few years, I have heard many stories of heartache, and each one tugs at my own heart. There is a similar thread woven through many of the accounts. That thread is faith being tested.

There are times when, although we pray for what we want, we understand and finally accept the Lord's will. Over the past few years, I have heard many stories of heartache, and each one tugs at my own heart. There is a similar thread woven through many of the accounts. That thread is faith being tested.

A typical story is that of Sonja, who wrote to say:

I didn't understand what faith was. In my mind, I thought that if I would have demonstrated enough faith, each of my four babies would have made it. After each loss, I tried harder to demonstrate my faith to Heavenly Father. I prayed more, I went to the temple more. Then, at some point during the pregnancy, I'd hear, "I'm sorry, your baby doesn't have a heartbeat. . . ." It was like being slapped in the face. I felt as though all of my efforts were being ignored.

It took me so long to understand that true faith includes accepting Heavenly Father's will in my life. It is turning to Him in times of despair. It is understanding and using the Atonement, not only to take away my sins but my sorrows as well.

Sonja's inspiring testimony reminds us that we often experience a different miracle than the one for which we prayed. Through faith and continual effort, we will learn lessons that otherwise we could never have experienced.

I got stuck on the "why?" for a long time. I really felt picked on. However, we continued to appear as though all was well. We came to church; we tried hard to smile. I appreciated having a supportive and loving husband, as well as caring family and friends.

Now I can look back and see that losing my babies actually saved me. It was a refiner's fire. Before the loss of my children, my self-esteem wasn't very high, and I was pretty lukewarm as far as my testimony was concerned. My testimony has grown, and I have found the courage to change (I think that courage comes from my little cheering section in heaven)!

It was a difficult time, true, with all of the pain,

the tears, and the guilt. But it has been worth the price I have had to pay to come to know my Heavenly Father.

Sonja's inspiring testimony reminds us that we often experience a different miracle than the one for which we prayed. Through faith and continual effort, we will learn lessons that otherwise we could never have experienced. Our Father in Heaven *does* know and love us, and He wants us to return to live with Him.

Often we reach for a miracle as we experience life's challenges, including seeking a healthier lifestyle. It can be frightening to step out of our comfort zone. But as we move forward, whatever our task, *we can do it!* It doesn't matter that we aren't the fastest runner.

However, no one can go through the refiner's fire for us. We must endure its heat for ourselves. As we seek to personally improve, keeping hope alive is essential. Even with the world's bright lights glaring and loud engines blaring, through faith, hard work, and acceptance of the Lord's hand in our lives, we can find our way on the road that leads to where we truly want to be.

Conclusion

I hope you have found hope and encouragement in these pages. Anyone who has experienced a few years of life knows that none of us is going to skate through mortality without a few, if not many, trials. That has been substantiated by the many women who have so generously shared their stories with me. Regardless of our righteousness, plans fail, expectations are dashed, and unexpected tragedies intrude. That has certainly been true in my life.

So, if we can't avoid trials and disappointments, what are we to do? Give up? Offer excuses? Spend our days feeling sorry for ourselves and asking why? Or are we going to move forward, accepting with patience that which life deals us and making the best of things?—looking forward with faith to the promised day when through the Atonement, "God shall wipe away all tears from [our] eyes; and there shall be no more death, neither sorrow, nor crying, neither shall there be any more pain: for the former things are passed away" (Revelation 21:4) and to the eternal blessings we have been promised.

I testify that if we have faith that Heavenly Father loves us, that the Savior understands our pain and will eventually remove it from us, and that the Holy Ghost will comfort and guide us through this veil of tears, there is still much joy to be had in living. My own experiences and the many stories included in this book are ample evidence of that.

So, if we can't avoid trials and disappointments, what are we to do? Give up? Offer excuses? Spend our days feeling sorry for ourselves and asking why? Or are we going to move forward, accepting with patience that which life deals us and making the best of things?

So, if you have allowed despair to rob you of joy and you are exhausted—tired of how you look, how you feel, and how you are living—please take heart. Things do not have to remain as they are.

The keys to change are:

• Exercise faith and be willing to work hard to make the necessary changes. The best time to start is NOW.
• Pray for strength, believing that desires of the flesh will diminish as you develop self-mastery.
• Never forget that faith makes miracles possible—physical, emotional, and spiritual miracles. Often, the miracle comes only after taking that first step ahead in the darkness or after having been through a hot refiner's fire.

Realize that we often experience a different miracle than the one for which we pray. Through faith and continual effort, we will learn lessons that otherwise we could never have experienced.

In conclusion, keep in mind this beautiful thought from our beloved President Gordon B. Hinckley: "I feel to invite women everywhere to rise to the great potential within you. I do not ask that you reach beyond your capacity. I hope you will not nag yourselves with thoughts of failure. I hope you will not try to set goals far beyond your capacity to achieve. I hope you will simply do what you can do in the best way you know. If you do so, you will witness miracles come to pass" (*Motherhood: A Heritage of Faith,* booklet [Salt Lake City: Deseret Book Co., 1995], 9).

That is my testimony as well.

About the Author

Pamela H. Hansen grew up in Salt Lake City, Utah. She attended the University of Utah and graduated from Brigham Young University with a degree in elementary education. She has taught first and second grades as well as adult ESL classes, although the majority of her life as a mother has been spent at home. She currently teaches weight loss/management classes at the Central Utah Clinic and also serves on the Women's Advisory Council, Utah Valley Regional Medical Center. She and her husband, Mark, live in Orem, Utah, where they are raising five children.

In her first book, *Running with Angels* (Shadow Mountain, 2005), Pam drew upon her experience of overcoming obesity and marathon running. She has completed three marathons and is featured in Fodor's *The Traveling Marathoner* (Fodor's Travel, Random House, 2006).

In 2005, Pam was awarded the "Matthew B. Roush Award

for Excellence in Contributions to Women's Health," given by the Women's Advisory Council, Utah Valley Regional Medical Center. She was also given the "Beacon of Hope Award" by the board of directors, Urban South Region, at Intermountain Health Care.

Running with Angels
5K Race

In 2005, the first annual Running with Angels 5K race was held. A partnership between Pam and Women's Services at Utah Valley Regional Medical Center, the race is a benefit run with proceeds going to provide scholarship funds for women wanting to improve their health, specifically with fitness and weight management health goals.

For more information on the race or to apply for scholarship funds, visit www.runningwithangels.com.